CW01082011

How To Profit
In
Up and Down Markets

BY

DOUG EBERHARDT

Dedicated to Mom and Dad

DISCLAIMER

Paperback ISBN 978-1-951250-00-3

Hardback ISBN 978-1-951250-02-7

CONTENTS

INTRODUCTION

Why do you invest the way you do? Is it because someone told you to invest that way and years from now, you will be simply fine if you "stick with the plan of buy and hold?" That is how most people invest. Who do you trust for investment advice, and why? Are they any good? How do you know? Have you compared them to any other advisors? How much do they make from their recommendations to you? How did they perform during the last fiscal crisis? What economic conditions occurring today can affect your wealth? How have you structured your portfolio differently to protect your wealth if we were to experience another economic downturn? What investment do you own to counter the potential of any potential downturn?

This book will answer those questions and provide you with the ability to either confidently make investments yourself or keep tabs of those who are managing your investments.

Most investors do not realize there are two sides of a market from which they can profit. Investors can profit from two sides of an individual stock, commodity, or currency. With the introduction of Exchange Traded Funds (ETFs) an investor is offered the opportunity to take more control of their wealth. Odds are your portfolio has no exposure to ETFs and more than likely no active strategies to protect you from any downturn in the market should it come. This is especially true if you have a 401(k) at your current employer. But even with a 401(k) you can utilize the information in this book to protect your portfolio in a prolonged down market.

Bear markets always come, and most financial advisors continue to keep investors in a buy and hold strategy, via the extremely popular index funds. Index Funds have no doubt worked well over the years, but could you have made more profit with a different type of strategy that allows you more control of your wealth? There are times when investors get hurt with the buy and hold strategy like they did during the 2007-2009 fiscal crisis. During those years most financial advisors spent their time fielding phone calls from disgruntled investors because their accounts were getting blown up. Investors were losing a good percentage of their wealth. This type of decline is coming again. But this time it can be a prolonged bear market that can last years (more on why later in this book), you can bank on it (that is your hint as to why a prolonged bear market is forthcoming)!

This book will bring you the tools and knowledge necessary to profit from the market whether you are an active or passive investor, while at the same time protecting your nest egg from the storms of economic and financial turmoil that always come. But unlike most financial advisors who use the same old buy and hold strategy, this book will allow you to manage your portfolio and profit more actively in both up and down markets. After reading this book, some of you may just fire your financial advisor!

There will still be some of you who need the guidance of a competent advisor, and this book will provide you with the questions you need to ask of them, to see if they know more than you do after reading this book. A trusted financial advisor is also needed as you grow older and get to the point where you need someone other than a family member to manage your affairs. But there is no reason you cannot take control today and beat the buy and hold market averages by following the advice laid out in this book.

"All wealth derives from knowledge." George Gilder, author, *Knowledge, and Power*

There are three types of wealth: income from employment, assets you have accumulated (real estate, stocks, bonds, mutual funds, CDs, annuities and possibly a family business), and inherited. Whether it is wealth you have accumulated over the years, or newfound wealth from a loved one passing away, your goal is the same; to invest wisely and have it grow while moving towards retirement, but also to keep it growing during retirement and most importantly protect it from market downturns. You should have more time on your hands in retirement to manage your wealth and this book will help. But what you will also see moving forward is the importance of maintaining your purchasing power from your wealth when most of your assets are tied up in US dollar-based investments. In fact, most of the time you will only need 15-30 minutes to prepare for the next trading day.

Knowing where we are in the cycle of investing in market sectors, commodities and bonds is one of the first steps to consider. Are we at the end of a bull cycle hitting new highs or completing a bear cycle where the market is hitting new lows, or somewhere in between? Is now the time to go buy or sell? You will know after reading this book. Yes, you can time the market with the right tools. All my books are about awareness and this book, being my third, is the one I am most proud of as it has taken a lifetime of mistakes to learn how not to repeat those mistakes.

It is not really that complicated to understand investing once you grasp the concept that there are two sides to every investment. You buy a stock and someone else is selling it. This book will explain the opportunities available that for decades have been only one sided, mostly because financial advisors have investors put their wealth into either mutual funds or index funds and sit back and take a nice fee for doing nothing but what the market does on its own.

Most investors go along the market with individual stocks, mutual funds or index funds and check in on their returns with their advisor every so often. They are passive investors and trust their advisor knows what they are doing, but their advisor is doing nothing that you cannot do on your own by tweaking your investment strategy.

For example, there are many ETFs available today to help you profit when the market falls. I will give you a secret; nothing goes straight up forever. Knowing where you are within the cycle will help you profit from both sides of the market moves, up or down. While this goes against investment advisor traditional thinking, well guess what? Most mutual funds these advisors sell cannot beat the market so one must really challenge the status quo thinking this day and age and you will see this book does in many ways. I have put 38 years into learning the markets and my prior books have challenged the status quo thinking over and over and this has led to many investors profiting from what I have written already. The strategies in this book top everything I have written before. Why? Because we evolve in our learning as to what works in the investment arena and this book will help you put on the armor you need to defend against the worldwide issues of potential wars, banking crisis', and any other calamity that may hit us again as Covid did, affecting millions of investors and businesses. If you had a signal to get you out of the falling stocks you were in, it would have saved you from losses. At the same time, you would have taken advantage of buying back stocks with some good strategies for entry.

The one thing the 2007–2009 fiscal crisis and the Covid crisis taught us is that stocks, bonds, mutual funds, hedge funds, real estate, and commodities like oil and gold are all illusions of wealth until you do one thing: lock in profit. Most financial advisors, economists, and those at the Federal Reserve did not see any of these crises coming. What makes anyone think they will see the next crisis coming? Wouldn't it be nice to know when to lock in profit on your successful investments? Most investors miss addressing this one important question, when to sell? Also, would it not be good to know when to cut your losses on a losing investment? If you follow the Trading Strategies section of this book, you will be able to do just that, and you will surprise yourself at your results compared to buy and hold strategies.

The market since 2009 has been in an unprecedented bull run fueled really by some tech giants like Apple, Amazon, Alphabet (formerly Google) Meta (formerly Facebook), Nvidia, sometimes Tesla and a few others. These companies make up most of the stock market return because they carry the most weight in the S&P 500 or Nasdaq as the largest companies. It is not a good representation of the strength of the overall market, which will be explained more later. And those who are in index funds need to know what the risks are with this heavily indexed weighting of a few companies of the index and how it can impact future returns.

What most do not understand about the strength of the current bull stock market run is that it has been fueled by Fed speculation on interest rates and extraordinary moves with quantitative easing in trying to boost the economy. If you throw trillions at the market, what do you expect to happen? The money must go somewhere, and it finds a way to fuel the stock market. But what consequences does it bring when you keep blowing air into a balloon? Eventually the air is let out.

As of now, the Fed has a balloon of over $7 trillion on their balance sheet. No one on CNBC addresses this as an issue. I have addressed it in my prior books, but kicking the can down the road only lasts if what is being kicked down the road, debt, does not get out of control. So far, the Fed has maintained a steady market despite some wicked up and down swings. What happens when they lose control? Notice I used the word "when" instead of if?

Remember, Janet Yellen in May of 2020 said, "I don't anticipate that inflation is going to be a problem." [1] Then it became one. The Fed said inflation was "transitory." Then the Fed had to begin a series of raising rates to fight inflation. The bond market got killed.

Even before that, in 2019, tariff talks put a damper on markets, or was it really the Fed raising rates when they should not have? Many times, the market trades simply on what the Fed says it will do, even without them doing it. The markets have become more volatile but are you making a profit?

The lesson to be learned by investors is that until they convert their wealth to cash or another asset, locking in profit, the value of each asset can and will swing wildly, depending on where it is in its investment cycle. Why not profit from both sides of that cycle? Even the safe haven known as the U.S. dollar swings wildly as it fell -10% in 2017. Two other times since 1985, the dollar fell -28% and -32%. This is supposed to be viewed as the "no risk" bedrock of your portfolio. The dollar could fall 30% more from here and most do not have any insurance against such a decline. Remember, if your portfolio goes up 30% and the dollar falls 30%, you have not gained any real purchasing power. Purchasing power is key.

Can you predict when the next black swan event that could erase much of the wealth you have accumulated is going to occur? This book will help you forecast what is to come but it is not one of those sky is falling types of books. There are always going to be ways to profit and quite frankly, an investor should not care what the economy does if they are on the right side of the market. A saying I like to use is I do not care what the market does if I am trading with the current trend, up and down. **And that is the key to this entire book.**

---

[1] https://ny1.com/nyc/all-boroughs/politics/2022/06/01/treasury-secretary-janet-yellen-i-was-wrong-about-inflation

Your financial advisor is typically brainwashed to think markets always go up and you cannot time the market. They say things like there are only a few days a year combined that if you missed, you would have missed the stock bull market run. The reality is, with the strategies in this book, you will not miss out. AND you will profit on the way down as the market falls too!

No matter the size of your portfolio and no matter what the economy is doing, you can benefit from trends in either direction with some trading rules and strategies set forth in this book. You will find that you can use this book as a guide for years to come. You will find the Trading Rules from the 1920's are still valid today and if you follow them and your trading plan you will do quite well.

This book will address many weaknesses we have as investors. One of the most critical issues facing investors early on is that our educational system, from high school to undergraduate and graduate school, simply does not instruct us on how to invest, let alone keep and grow wealth. Heck, it does not even teach us about the dollar which is what our whole monetary system is based on.

We either count on financial advisors, insurance agents, and money managers to make us money or we are left to our own devices—if we are lucky enough to have the time to do the necessary research. This book will save you time and money in providing you with answers you need today, to prepare for the volatility of these markets and profit no matter what the market does. But you must possess the knowledge of where we are in the current cycle among other criteria before getting comfortable. The more awareness you possess, the more you will be able to put the pieces together for yourself better than most financial advisors can and that is what this book will help with. After reading this book, think about giving it to your children so they can learn the techniques to profit from an early age. Their teachers will not provide this type of knowledge to them. Only you can.

You will know after reading this book if you are equipped to manage your own wealth, by going it alone—and saving the fees and commissions that advisors typically take from your bottom line, or if you need to seek a professional advisor.

As people live longer and longer it is more important today than ever to keep as much of your wealth as possible, and to make the extra effort to understand how to grow it. You can read magazines that tell you about the latest hot investment or take some advice from some X (formerly known as Twitter) guru, only to have that investment reverse course by the time you buy it. Or you can leave your money decisions to your advisor who takes commissions from your retirement nest egg with simple buy and hold and index fund advice. Or you can take the best route for your investment future and follow the insight that stands the test of time that this book provides. I have backtracked and applied the knowledge of this book to convince myself first that it works before releasing it to the public. I have spent four years revising it. I am confident in what I have written and that is why I am sharing it with you.

There are some of you out there that just want the shortcut to everything. That is why YouTube or TiKTok videos are so popular now instead of taking the time to read a book. Lazy investors want answers quickly on how to trade successfully so they can get straight to profit taking. There are no shortcuts to trading, but if I was forced to give you one or two and you do not want to read an entire book to understand investments, go straight to the Technicals section under Trading Strategies in this book. Follow the guidelines there on what to look for and how to set up your charts and have at it. But also copy the Trading Rules to go along with it. But having an overall understanding of markets I think makes you a better investor and I provide that. You'll make less mistakes and control your emotions and greed with sound, proven strategies that work.

For some of you, it really can be that simple. This can work for new investors too as it will drive you to go out and make more money to invest as you will see your success in investing transform your life. Most advisors do not like dealing with someone with limited funds but that does not have to stop you from taking control of your future with sound investment strategies as the money comes in.

Read this book from beginning to end and get a feel for what to look for when trading before diving into the technical side of things. Of course, I do offer a trading service at the end of this book because yes, a little guidance of when to buy and sell does not hurt. Try it for a month or two for the small cost and see what some proven strategies can do to improve your investing results.

For that matter, all my books have been about awareness. I wrote a gold and silver book and sell gold and silver investments and it is amazing that gold keeps breaking to new highs. How did I know that would occur? In that gold investment book, I expose how most of the other companies selling gold and silver charge extremely high commissions through TV and radio advertisements. I offer gold and silver investments that are much cheaper and I am proud of it. I'm offering a trading service where I want you, the investor, to be aware of what to "think" before you invest so you are on the right side of the market, and what I charge for this awareness is much cheaper than what a financial advisor would charge.

Can a single book transform your investment life? I think it can.

PART 1 – KNOWING YOUR ADVISORS:
QUESTIONS TO ASK, PAST PERFORMANCE, CRITIQUE AND HIDDEN AGENDAS

CHAPTER 1 - PREPARING TO INTERVIEW YOUR FINANCIAL ADVISOR

Seeking Financial Advice

Investors turn to financial advisors to learn how to best manage and grow their portfolios. Novice investors inquire about how to plan for their future. How did you first come by your advisor? Was it a recommendation from a friend or relative? Did you call someone because you heard a radio or television commercial or read an ad in a magazine? Did you do a search on the internet for a local advisor? Were you cross sold on investing in something an insurance agent?

When it comes to picking an advisor, or even making sure your current advisor is up to the task of managing your portfolio in *your* best interest, it is important to ask certain questions to justify either hiring or keeping them as your investment counselor moving forward. Their answers to the questions that follow in the pages ahead will give you the confidence you need to choose or retain the right advisor. Simply put, if they do not know more than you do after you have read this book, then why should they manage your investments?

Even with this scrutiny, it does not hurt to get a second or even a third opinion from one or more additional advisors. This is your money, and your wealth—it is your responsibility to choose a competent advisor who will make sure you can keep and grow it.

I know from experience in selling gold and silver that most who buy precious metals do so because they saw an ad on TV or heard an ad on radio. The person who answers the phone typically convinces them to buy high commission coins. These investors do not look around or take the time to read a book on investing in metals. Next thing you know they are down 30% on their investment.

You need to do some research before doing anything and know who you are buying from and to whom you are sending your investment capital. Or better, figure out how to do it yourself. That is the holy grail for you as an investor; to take control of your wealth. You will see that as a central theme of this book.

It also may even make sense to have more than one advisor manage your wealth, dividing up your assets among them. Most advisors will try to manage your entire portfolio because the more they manage, the more they can potentially make. But splitting up your investments among a few advisors might benefit you, depending on the size of your portfolio.

In 2016, we had record fines from brokerage firms amounting to $175 million. The next 3 years fines were between $40 and $70 million per year. In 2021 we jumped to $103 million and 2022 $111 million with 2023 coming in at $90 million. There we were back to up around $89 trillion. [2]

It is important now more than ever to check up on your advisor. You can check your broker with this link: https://brokercheck.finra.org/

Questions to Ask of Yourself and Your Financial Advisor

When seeking investment advice from the advisors you have selected to interview, you need to adopt a fearless mindset. Some advisors may object to you asking these questions, and if they do, they are not suited to managing your money. Simply take control from the beginning and ask if it is ok to ask a few questions before you get started. Write down the answers or ask if you can record the interview for the protection of both parties. By taking control and doing this first, you will weed out those who are just there to sell you something or lack the necessary knowledge of their own industry or have the skills you can put your trust in. Remember, it is more than likely illegal to record someone without their permission. Always ask for permission first.

---

[2] https://www.investmentnews.com/regulation-and-legislation/news/finra-fines-spike-63-in-2023-report-250732

Before the advisor interview, answer these questions yourself before doing any interviews.

Questions You Need to Answer for <u>Yourself</u> Before Interviewing Your Advisor

1. If the interviewee is a family friend, are they someone you trust with all your investment planning?
2. Would it hurt to get a second opinion from one or two additional candidates?
3. Do you feel uncomfortable investing in something you do not understand fully?
4. What type of investor are you: short-term or long-term investor, swing trader, value investor? Are your investment goals conservative, moderate, aggressive? A good advisor will ask before recommending investments.
5. Eighty percent of the mutual fund managers do not beat their related indices. Is your advisor going to just put you in indexed mutual funds or ETFs?
6. Do financial advisors add value?
7. Are you afraid to fire your current financial advisor?
8. Does your advisor have a verifiable track record?
9. Is your advisor professional in appearance? Organized? Confident in his recommendations?

<u>General Questions to Ask Your Advisor</u> (Important: Sizing up your advisor as one who has your best interest or someone who wants to sell you something they make a nice commission from sets advisors apart).

1. Is there a charge for this consultation? (Most advisors will not charge you as the companies compensate them .
2. Do you work strictly on commissions or a percentage of assets, or a flat fee? (Commissioned advisors will push products they make the most money on. Most will still charge you fees no matter what the market does.)

3. Will you tell me exactly how much you make from any investment you recommend? (Insurance agents will balk at this or say something like, "there are no fees to you" when in fact they make a huge commission built into the product they sell.)
4. Is your fee or commission negotiable? (Just like with a real estate agent, fees can be negotiated, especially if you are investing a large amount.)
5. Will you charge me a fee if my investments lose money for the year? It is possible to get fees waived in such a case, but it must be written into the contract.
6. Do you sell stocks, bonds, ETFs, mutual funds, and REITs, or are you limited to selling products from the insurance industry, which would include annuities and cash value life insurance? (You want to find out if they are only a licensed insurance agent pushing high commission annuities or life products – see insurance chapter)
7. Will you try and sell me your own company's stock or proprietary products, because you are paid extra bonuses or commissions? (Big firms will not like this question as there are always incentives to sell their proprietary products, including trips to exotic places. Insurance agents are especially pushing certain annuities over others to qualify to win trips.)
8. How often will we be reviewing my portfolio? (This will vary from advisor to advisor, but a phone call quarterly and face to face meeting once a year is in order.)
9. Can I ask for three references from clients you have worked with? (They should be willing to provide.)
10. Have you ever had any disciplinary action against you? (You can check on an advisor by going here to the FINRA (Financial Industry Regulatory Authority): https://www.finra.org/#/

Investment Advice Questions for Your Advisor

1. Will you ask me any questions to decipher what kind of investor I am? (Conservative, moderate, aggressive.)
2. How did you do in advising clients before and after the 2007–2009 fiscal crisis or during the Covid crisis? (If they kept clients' portfolios fully invested in stocks during that entire move lower, then see #4 below)
3. How has your financial advice changed to protect clients from any potential future stock or bond market crash? (This is where a buy and hold advisor will argue to hold through everything and this book may teach you otherwise.)
4. What type of protection does your advice offer against any downturn in stocks? (Insurance agents say have the ideal product, but it is not – See insurance chapter)
5. What penalty will there be if, after investing with you, I want to liquidate my account the next day after I invest with you? (Get this in writing as this question gets to the heart of how they might be compensated.)
6. Do you sell Real Estate Investment Trusts (REITs)? Some advisors will sell these but there are liquidity risks they should explain to you as you will not be able to get your money out at any time. During and after Covid, many investors lost much of their principal investment in commercial real estate REIT's. They had no way to get out. By the time they got out they had lost a good chunk of the investment.
7. Do you base your investment recommendations on asset allocation strategies? (You will learn more about this later, but you want to buy low and sell high and need to see if the advisor knows where we are in the current investment cycle and what strategies they will implement to protect the downside, if any.)
8. Will my portfolio maintain its purchasing power over time if the dollar loses value? (Many will not be able to answer this question. Typically, their answer will be to invest in TIPS (Treasury Inflation bonds). You should expect more out of

your advisor than just this solution. This scenario will be addressed in this book.

9. Where are you (the advisor) personally invested right now? (See if this compares to the recommendations they present to you. Can save this question till after they make recommendations to see if they – put their money where their mouth is.)

Economic and Monetary Quiz

If you want to dig even deeper into what your advisor knows, which you should also be aware of if you have read any of my books, ask them these questions before allowing them to manage your money. It will give you an idea as to their knowledge base.

1. What is the current national debt? 2019 over $22.5 trillion. 2023, $33.7 trillion) 2024 over $34 trillion.
2. What is the current budget deficit? A2019, $1 Trillion. 2023 $1.7 trillion. 2024 $1.6 trillion
3. What backs the U.S. dollar? (answer: full faith and credit of the US government but it is the power of the US military).
4. What are your views on owning physical gold and silver? (This question is to see if they are like many advisers who do not recommend this asset class without really knowing why it is important to maintaining purchasing power, described later in this book).

Are Financial Advisors Needed?

If you are getting up there in age and do not have a family member to help with the management of your portfolio—or you simply do not have the time to pay attention to your investments, a trusted advisor is invaluable and necessary.

Also, if you are older, you may need some guidance in making investment management decisions. Having a financially competent friend or relative present during the meeting with potential advisors or sitting alongside you during your next meeting with your present advisor makes sense. This may be difficult for those who like to keep financial matters private from family members or friends. But by including a trusted close relative or friend in making investment decisions, you can help protect your wealth and at the same time avoid getting ripped off by some fast-talking, likable advisor who charms investors into turning over their money to them to manage and take large commissions from or worse. Also know who you are giving the durable power of attorney to in managing your affairs when you cannot any longer. This should be discussed with your attorney.

Most of us do not do the extra homework to manage our own investments. Even those who think they can professionally manage their own investments by day trading or timing investments typically learn the hard way that they do not possess the necessary skills to profit, and they lose money—sometimes a lot of money.

After reading this book and going through the process of asking questions of your advisor you will be able to discern whether a financial advisor adds value. If professional money managers and hedge fund managers cannot beat the indices, then what value does a financial advisor add if they are just going to put you in an index fund and get paid fees for doing so? Yes, there are some good advisors out there and they can bring added value to your overall financial plan if they have the extra designations like a Certified Financial Planner can bring. They have gone the extra step to educate themselves and you should go the extra step to make sure your advisor has this designation if your portfolio deems it. You just need to do your homework to find them, and it starts with interviewing them and asking the right questions. A CFP will pass with excellence.

CHAPTER 2 - PERFORMANCE OF MUTUAL FUND AND HEDGE FUND MANAGERS

The Truth about Mutual Fund and Hedge Fund Managers' Performance

Are you invested in actively managed mutual funds? Many of you were told to buy these investments because some financial advisor recommended you do so. The harsh reality is that those of you in the U.S. who own 90% of the $17 trillion held in mutual funds did not beat the market index. The same is true for the rest of the world investors who invest an additional $16 trillion in mutual funds.

The United States Has the World's Largest Mutual Fund and ETF Markets
Percentage of total net assets, year-end 2014

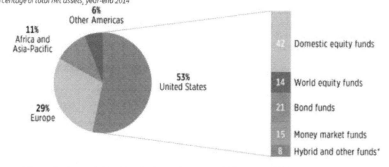

Total worldwide mutual fund and ETF assets: $33.4 trillion   Total U.S. mutual fund and ETF assets: $17.8 trillion

* Includes ETFs—both registered and not registered under the Investment Company Act of 1940—that invest primarily in commodities, currencies, and futures.
Note: Components may not add to 100 percent because of rounding.
Sources: Investment Company Institute and International Investment Funds Association

The real truth when it comes to this professional manager performance is for the 9 years prior to 2019, the majority of large-cap funds lagged the S&P 500 with 85% of large-cap funds under performing, and the last 15 years prior to 2019, 92% trailed the index.[3] With a success rate of 8%15 how are mutual funds still in business? Why would anyone put their money in mutual funds with

---

[3] https://www.cnbc.com/2019/03/15/active-fund-managers-trail-the-sp-500-for-the-ninth-year-in-a-row-in-triumph-for-indexing.html

that kind of underperformance record? Yet we see over $33 trillion of wealth invested there as of that time. Through 2022, not one of 2,132 actively managed stock or bond mutual funds outperformed the market convincingly and regularly. In 2023, 60% of all active large-cap U.S. equity funds lagged the S&P 500. [456]

Is it any wonder index funds took over for managed mutual funds?

When you add the fees that mutual fund managers make, it takes even more away from your overall return. Mutual funds have raised their fees from an average of 0.62 % of assets to 1.11%, an increase of 84%.[7]

When I was in the business of selling mutual funds, the fund managers set up incentives or rewards for brokers to sell their funds. I won a mink coat for my mother by being the first to sell a million in mutual funds with a company I represented. I have attended Linsco Private Ledger conferences (LPL), the largest independent brokerage firm in the U.S., with the most independent brokers working for them. The mutual fund companies were at these conferences wining and dining the brokers, taking them to private suites at baseball games, private catered events at local restaurants they would rent out for the night and setting up intimate concerts with top name performers. They hired Sheryl Crow and have hired others like Hootie and the Blow Fish and Lionel Richie recently to perform for a small group of attendees. This is where those fees go!

The fees are even higher when you wrap an annuity with a mutual fund. The trips these brokers compete for when selling these products are first class all the way. I won a trip for two to Ireland at the 5-star hotel The Berkley Court, complete with dinner at a castle with our own private quartet playing music for us. Brokers are treated like kings and queens at these events. But the performance of the

---

[4] https://www.nytimes.com/2022/12/02/business/stock-market-index-funds.html

[5] https://www.morningstar.com/funds/active-funds-fell-short-passive-peers-2023

[6] https://www.nytimes.com/2022/12/02/business/stock-market-index-funds.html

[7] http://www.forbes.com/sites/robertlenzner/2013/05/30/mutual-funds-biting-the-dust-at-an-alarming-rate/

ones paying for this royalty treatment of brokers cannot outperform the market 90% of the time. I have not worked for these types of companies for 30 years but enjoyed it at the time. Naturally, investors have done well in the last 30 years in most of the investments sold and unfortunately while the rewards may still be there for advisors to enjoy, the investor moving forward should not expect the same performance and this will be explained later in this book as to why.

Which brings us to an interesting point I would like to make here: If you invested $50,000 in a Vanguard index fund (we discuss Index Funds in depth later as a viable alternative to mutual fund investing) with an average expense ratio of 0.19%, in 30 years you would have $65,793 more than someone who invested in a fund with the industry average expense ratio of 1.11%.[8] You can pay for your own royalty treatment for your own trips and concerts for yourself with those kinds of savings.

FINRA has a good calculator you can use to see the fees your mutual fund is charging you. It can be found at https://tools.finra.org/fund_analyzer/

Mutual fund sales are big business, and financial advisors make good commissions from selling these actively managed funds to you. But are they really working in your best interest in doing so? I do not think so, and the data proves it. What did you pay to get into your current mutual fund? To answer this, you need to know what type of shares you bought: "A," front load; "B," back-end load (charged upon redemption, but reduced typically by 1% a year); "C," annual fees (sometimes called no-load funds); and "H," which is a hybrid of "A" and "B" that includes both a smaller front load and back-end load.[9] On a $10,000 investment in A shares, a 5% front-load fee would be $500. This means you start your investment with $9,500, but there are no back-end fees upon liquidation. When you purchase B shares, you pay fees if you were to liquidate your investment. With B shares you are charged a declining fee that typically starts at 5% and disappears after five to seven years, depending on the fund.

[8] https://personal.vanguard.com/us/insights/article/mutual-fund-costs-122013
[9] http://www.icifactbook.org/pdf/13_fb_table62.pdf

C shares, or no-load funds, typically charge an annual fee—known as a 12b-1—that amounts to 0.25% of the fund's average annual net assets. It is important to note that B back-end load shares also have a 12b-1 fee associated with them.

Most all these annual commission fees go to your broker.

Below you will find a comparison of three large-cap blend funds with A shares represented by Rydex Funds (RYTTX), B shares represented by Prudential (PTMBX), and a no-load fund represented by Vanguard (VFIAX). The purpose of this analysis is not to say one fund outperforms the other based on how the manager invests, but to show you how fees and commission charged can affect your overall total return. Each fund has an initial investment of $20,000, the same 10-year timeframe, and an assumed annual return of 7%. You see why it is important to ask how your advisor gets paid? No load funds clearly won out.

Large Cap Fund	Fees & Commissions 10 Years	Redeemed Fund Value Minus Expenses After 10 Years
Vanguard 500 Index Fund Admiral Class [VFIAX] (No Load)	$142.55	$39,146.82
Rydex Series Trust Dynamic S&P 500 Fund Class A [RYTTX] (Front Load)	$5,301.58	$31,426.95
Prudential Large Cap Core Equity Fund Class B [PTMBX] (Back Load)	$4,314.41	$33,109.84

All things being equal, you can see how lower fees can make an enormous difference to your overall return. You should be aware of what your advisor is selling you and ask about fees.

Also know that financial advisors still push mutual funds on investors as they have grown from $16 trillion under management to $28 trillion as of 2022. 2023 saw investors move away from active managers in all categories showing that passive fund managers like the Vanguard Index Fund which controls 30% of the market being the main beneficiaries.[10][11]

[10] https://www.morningstar.com/funds/recovery-us-fund-flows-was-weak-2023
[11] https://www.morningstar.com/funds/recovery-us-fund-flows-was-weak-2023

Hedge Fund Investors have had
Worse Returns than Mutual Funds

Hedge fund returns have been worse than mutual funds lately. There are over 10,000 hedge funds holding $2.4 trillion in assets, but hedge funds only rose 7.4% on average in 2013, making it the fifth straight year that hedge fund managers have not beat the S&P 500.[12] The simple investment in the S&P 500 Index has outperformed hedge funds for 10 straight years except for 2008 when the S&P lost big. But that particular year hedge fund managers edged out mutual fund managers in overall performance.[13]

Let us compare the past few years of hedge fund returns.

The best hedge fund manager of 2013 was David Tepper of Appaloosa Management. His fund was up approximately 38%, or just 9% above the S&P 500 Index. For this performance, Tepper was paid $3 billion.[14]

Just imagine what the hedge fund managers who are not beating the index are getting paid! According to a recent Citibank study,[15] it is estimated that hedge fund managers need at least $300 million Assets Under Management (AUM) to break even. This would mean that of the $300 million total needed for expenses, an investment manager would receive about 20% of $60 million, or $18 million, even before the fund has made a dime. For investors, the larger the fund, the less the manager makes. But of course, that is on a much larger piece of the pie.

---

[12] http://ww.businessweek.com/news/2014-01-07/hedge-funds-rise-7-dot-4-percent-in-2013-to-trail-s-and-p-500-for-fifth-year

[13] http://www.economist.com/news/finance-and-economics/21568741-hedge-funds-have-had-another-lousy-year-cap-disappointing-decade-going

[14] http://nypost.com/2013/12/29/hedge-fund-titan-to-pocket-3b-for-2013/

[15]

http://www.citibank.com/icg/global_markets/prime_finance/docs/2013_Business_Expense_Benchmark_Survey.pdf

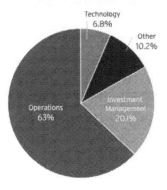

The wealthy in America may impress their friends by saying "I invest in hedge funds," but clearly most that do so are worse off than anyone else. Hedge funds have underperformed the S&P 500 every year since 2008 until 2018, when they beat the S&P but still ended the year with a loss.

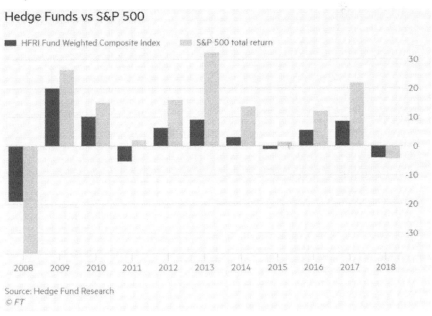

Hedge Funds vs S&P 500

Source: Hedge Fund Research
© FT

In 2019 the average hedge fund return was 10.67% and the S&P returned 31.49%. In 2020 the average hedge fund return was 10.29% and the S&P 500 returned 18.40%. 2021 saw the average hedge fund return at 7.60% and the S&P 500 rose 26.89%. Actively managed large-cap U.S. stock funds fared better against the S&P 500 in 2022 but still had a 51% rate of underperformance according to a scorecard report from S&P Dow Jones Indices. In 2023, Hedge funds in 2023 averaged a 5.7% return in the year through November, according to hedge fund research firm PivotalPath. Equities and credit-focused strategies were the best performers, while macro and managed futures lagged. By contrast, the S&P 500 index rose over 20%.[16][17]

Why are you paying someone to manage your money when it is clear, overall, that you have a higher probability of success by simply buying an index fund with lower fees? Which investment will put more money in *your* retirement account instead of your brokers pocket?

Of course, it is not as simple as that. Proper asset allocation is needed, along with some built-in protection from unknown forces that can bring a repeat of a fiscal crisis that took everyone by surprise in 2007–2009 and again during the Covid crisis and once again in 2022.

You are now informed as to how well "the professionals" are doing with your hard-earned money. It is not a pretty picture. Yet investors flock to mutual funds and hedge funds instead of buying an index.

Breaking Up Is Hard to Do

An investor needs to know how to break up with the financial advisor who is telling them to invest in mutual funds and hedge funds that do not beat the market. Personally, liking an advisor does not mean you need to stay with them if they continually lose you money or cannot even beat the S&P 500 Index. You must choose your financial future over friendship.

---

[16] https://www.morningstar.com/news/marketwatch/20240306263/for-the-14th-year-in-a-row-the-sp-500-did-better-than-the-majority-of-actively-managed-us-large-cap-stock-funds

[17] https://www.morningstar.com/news/marketwatch/20240306263/for-the-14th-year-in-a-row-the-sp-500-did-better-than-the-majority-of-actively-managed-us-large-cap-stock-funds

PART 2 - INVESTING

CHAPTER 3 – START WITH UNDERSTANDING INVESTMENT BASICS

Understanding What You Are Doing

Whether you go it alone or have a team of qualified advisors, or both, the awareness this section brings will help you navigate the choppy investment waters ahead. You will be free to change course and chart a new path to investing with a higher degree of confidence. Once you take the emotion of uncertainty out of investing, you are left with enlightenment and profit.

A good many investors typically invest the wrong way. They hear about an investment that keeps going higher and higher and then FOMO (Fear of Missing Out) takes over. They finally make the move and allocate a portion of their wealth to that investment and soon what occurs? The investment goes the other way against them.

The problem lies in the fact that the investment they just put their funds into was overbought by the time they first heard about it. After the investment goes lower, they think to themselves, "I'm just a lousy investor," when they just did not look at the big picture as to where that investment was in relation to its average or mean price. To put it bluntly, they were just lazy or, to give them some credit, did not know how to do a little research before investing.

If you are lazy with your investment research before buying anything, or do not know what research to do, you reap what you sow. Investors need to take the laziness out of investing and have a plan. Then investors can be proactive with their investing and be confident with their trades.

Cycle Analysis

Knowing where a sector you want to invest in is in relationship to its historic mean will give you the ability to garner more profit. Every sector has a cycle, and where you are in that cycle matters most. But our psychological makeup does not allow us to buy what is beaten down. We forget the golden rule of "buy low and sell high," and we just follow the masses over the cliff of market losses that always seems to come at the top of a sector in bubble territory. Always place your investment choices or current allocation into the following cycle chart and you will have more opportunity to profit.

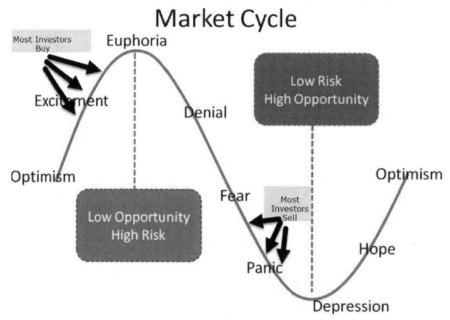

An investor can lose wealth quickly if they do not know what they are doing. Most investors do not have a plan. It is like the new gambler going to Las Vegas, not knowing the rules while playing blackjack and hitting on a 13, 14, 15 or 16 when the dealer is showing 3, 4, 5, or the six card face up. Odds are the dealer will bust with those numbers, but if you take his bust card, the rest of the players at the table are not going to be happy with you.

With your own hard-earned money, why are you gambling without knowing what you are really doing? The market makers are just like the Vegas dealers and are more than happy to take your money and will. But the deck does not have to be stacked against you as you can also trade *with* the professionals.

There are always two sides to trade, and the world is full of novice investors who simply do not take the time to learn before they earn. You do not make money by dipping your toes into a certain investment strategy without practicing first. Whether it be trading simulators that are like actual trading that most brokerage houses offer, or paper trading, pretending to buy and sell an investment, taking profit and keeping stops if it goes against you, one can practice trading before putting their real money at risk. Have a plan and work on your plan. But first, know where your market cycle is for what investment you are buying. Know the big picture. The rest is to look for other signals to convince you to buy or sell or stay away.

Having a Trading Plan

But before you get into simulated trading, you must have a trading plan. After you read the section on Trading Strategies, you will have a plan to trade every time.

Research Before You Invest

While this book is a good source for knowing more about investing and holding on to your wealth while growing it, I spend every day looking at the headlines and reading stories from CNBC, *The Financial Times*, *The Wall Street Journal*, Seeking Alpha, MarketWatch, *USA Today*, Yahoo, CNN, Investors Business Daily and other media sources. I also listen to many podcasts on the markets and read the alternative media that is always negative on the economy and predicts doom and gloom constantly, like ZeroHedge. Lastly, I peruse X (formerly known as Twitter), Instagram, Tiktoc and Facebook reels for the latest trends beyond what the data shows.

I like to hear from other investors around the world, so I make comments on articles to engage others and see what I might be missing. But what much of the media above does is just get investors to jump on an investment while the smart investor has already been long. The smart investor is selling to the new investor. How do you become a smart investor?

Risk

Before you make an investment, you want to know what risks are associated with it. Depending on the nature of the investment, the following potential risks need to be considered:

1. Liquidity risk - If everyone runs for the exit at the same time, you need buyers to sell to. If buyers are not there by the time you want to exit, the price may be lower than you expected. Selling real estate in a declining market and selling your hedge fund position where the hedge fund managers may halt liquidation to save some of the assets in the fund from being sold at large losses are two areas to watch out for. REIT's for example, are illiquid and many got killed during the Covid crisis. Before investing, know your ability to exit is paved with enough volume and liquidity.

2. Interest rate risk - When interest rates move higher, your bond funds will lose principal.

3. Inflation risk - Make sure you invest in areas that will automatically compensate for inflation when inflation rears its ugly head as it has since 2022. Inflation risk is here to stay.

4. Geographic risk - Emerging markets that have high debt levels will be a difficult area to be long in a declining market. Look for the lowest Debt to GDP countries to buy the dip in. Argentina in the last 5 years has seen the peso to dollar go from 50 to 350 in 2022 and over 900 in 2024. Their debt went from 50% of GDP to over 100% during this period. A new President who is making necessary cuts to government is a good thing but is it too late? What could they have done to counter this potential risk before the peso crashed? What other countries are in the same boat today?

5. Natural disaster risk - weather seems to be getting worse everywhere (whether manufactured or natural). Flooding, hurricanes, typhoons, and drought wreak so much havoc that even insurance companies are packing up and leaving affected areas like State Farm and others have in California.[18]

---

[18] https://www.kiplinger.com/personal-finance/home-insurance/state-farm-to-exit-homeowner-renewal-policies-in-california

6. Geopolitical risk – Brexit, change of leadership, ISIS, al Qaeda, Russia/Ukraine, Taiwan/China/US, Hamas/Isreal wars, or threat of war in retaliation leading to more Middle East issues, terrorist activity hotspots, open borders, coup d'état can all effect your investment. All these events should be watched closely and their potential effects on buy and hold strategies that can flip against you.

7. Central Bank Policy – central banks around the world are continually manipulating interest rates to either bring inflation or reduce inflation to levels they deem, as necessary. Yet as pointed out earlier, Treasury Secretary Janet Yellen did not anticipate inflation to be a problem in May of 2021, said it was transitory, only to regret saying it after inflation moved higher into 2024. [19]

8. To think the Federal Reserve will get inflation back to 2% again is pure fantasy. Inflation jumped to 8.5% in 2022 and has come back down but is still elevated and higher than the Fed's mandate of 2%. Real inflation versus the government's version of inflation shows an even higher number. The government has social security payment increases tied to the CPI, so they keep changing the makeup of the CPI to keep it artificially low. Using the old way of calculating the CPI has inflation over 10%. [20]

Bear Markets

Baby Boomers have fueled this stock market, and the going's been good overall for investors since 2009. But these Boomers also have fresh in their memories the 2009 market crash, and at any sign of trouble will move out of the stock market, as they cannot afford to take another hit like the last one. You do not want to be the last one out, but we can look at market tops and valuations and make some assumptions. However, the signals you will learn in the Trading

---

[19] https://www.kiplinger.com/personal-finance/home-insurance/state-farm-to-exit-homeowner-renewal-policies-in-california

[20] https://www.fedsmith.com/2023/04/19/inflation-severity-depends-how-its-measured/

Strategies section will make you not care if it is a bear or bull market. You will be on the right side of it, living your life rather than worrying about the future. This kind of peace of mind is how investing should be.

Also, adding trillions of dollars of government spending keeps the game going longer as money finds a home in stocks. When the excess spending dries up, watch out. [21] Even Elon Musk says America is heading for bankruptcy. [22]

Simulated Trading – Practice before you invest.

I mentioned before to practice some of the trading concepts in this book and want to discuss this a bit further. There are some good stock market simulators out there that make sense for you to play around with—using paper money before your hard-earned money is invested. These simulators allow you to trade a stock/ETF or multiple stocks/ETFs and trade them as if you were trading live with the market. If you were to practice doing this for a month, it would give you an idea of whether you are ready to risk your own money.

I will throw out one caution: If you practice your trading or even go to live trading in a bull market, almost any investment moves higher, and you will look brilliant with your choices. But when the market turns south, investing becomes much more difficult. What worked before with a bull market may not work in a bear market. It is important to understand the trend and trade in its direction.

You can check with your current online broker if they have a stock simulator, but some good ones can be found below. I am partial to Charles Schwab's think-or-swim using the indicators I provide in this book.

> thinkorswim paperMoney® from Charles Schawb (formerly TD Ameritrade)
> https://www.schwab.com/learn/story/thinkorswim-papermoney-stock-trading-simulator

---

[21] https://www.usbank.com/investing/financial-perspectives/market-news/how-do-rising-interest-rates-affect-the-stock-market.html

[22] https://twitter.com/elonmusk/status/1816814086149005495

Market Watch VSE http://www.marketwatch.com/game/

Investopedia http://www.investopedia.com/simulator/

Wall Street Survivor http://www.wallstreetsurvivor.com/

Important Note: One thing an online stock trading simulator will not do is allow your emotions to enter the picture. It is only through live trading with your own money that emotions get in the way of your trading. Remember, having a trading plan eliminates emotions. The market will dictate your moves with a trading plan.

Chapter 4 - More Investment Basics to Understand, Practicing Patience, Diversification, High-Frequency and Algo Trading, Shorting the Market

Practicing Patience

Patience works both ways; knowing when to sell and when to buy. One can be too early and buy a falling investment or they become greedy and refuse to lock in profit and the investment begins a freefall and they hold on to the investment thinking it will come back and they can get out with profit. Then it keeps falling and falling and they hold on just trying to get even. Then, as we saw in the market cycle graph earlier, they give up on the investment just when it is bottoming out and sell. Wouldn't it be nice to have a plan and buy and sell the investment at the right time?

Some investors may become concerned that their money is earning nothing sitting in cash or a money market account and want to deploy funds to jump on trending stocks that are already near their highs. Boredom sinks in and again FOMO enters the picture. But the patient investor simply waits for the right opportunity.

Good investors develop a feel for the market. They wait for the "panic" to develop in the market cycle, and they cost average into their allocation, which we will discuss in a bit. The smart investor then simply waits for the inevitable rebound in that sector. Patience is rewarded.

High-Frequency Trading or Artificial Intelligence (AI)

Are you smarter than a computer? Can computers come in and trade your portfolio better than you ever could? It sure would make life easier if you could utilize this technology and be profitable.

Most investors think of computer trading as the type of programmed trading done by computers by big Wall Street firms, where stocks are bought and sold in masse when certain price levels are hit. Most of us small investors are not privy to such technology. But lately there has been a growing trend toward computerized trading that may be putting some investment advisors out of business.

We have already shown that most mutual fund and hedge fund managers cannot beat the market and why paying their fees typically does not make sense for investors. One could just invest in an index, or, just like the computer that wins at chess all the time against a human, a computer can do better at predicting trends.

Large investment firms (including Vanguard, Charles Schwab, Blackrock and even on the insurance side, Northwestern Mutual) have entered the automated trading arena. If big money is behind it, you know there is some validity there.

An algorithmic trading investment approach is not for everyone, but there is a niche it can fill for those who have no time, are new to investing, or do not want to pay high fees for advice.

Is this type of trading for you? One of the companies, AlgoTrades, offers a quiz to find out.[23]

Answer the statements below with a YES or NO answer. Add up the total numbers of Yes's	YES	NO
Are you an active trader?	O	O
Are you a casual investor?	O	O
Are you tired of watching your account decline during market down turns and bear markets?	O	O
Do you have a detailed investment plan to work from?	O	O
Do you currently have a financial advisor managing your money?	O	O
Do you have clear trade and investment criteria for new position and position management?	O	O
Use a protective stop on every trade to limit losses in the event of a selloff or market crash?	O	O
Do you try to manage your own investments?	O	O
Do you have trading rules but do not stick too?	O	O
Do you have a routine that gets you back on track when you're trading is off?	O	O
Do your losing investments typically out-weigh your winners?	O	O
Do you have having several winning trades, followed by larger crash and burn type of trades?	O	O
Do you experience hesitation, apprehension, uncertainty, or fear when you are about to trade?	O	O
Do you double-down after a losing streak or when you're losing to re-gain profits faster?	O	O
Have you ever experienced the "I don't care" mode and watched your money disappear?	O	O
Were you successful in another profession and find trading is affecting your confidence and ego?	O	O
Do you lose sleep over your trading and investments?	O	O
Are you exiting positions too quickly instead of waiting for its full potential?	O	O
Do you want your positions managed properly for maximum profit potential?	O	O
Are a high percentage of your trades defensive?	O	O
You logically know what to do in a trade but find you are not taking the actions you should?	O	O

---

[23] http://www.algotrades.net/wp-content/uploads/2013/10/1MinuteQuiz.pdf

If you add up the total number of "YES" answers and it is more than six, they say an automated trading system is for you, and it is "risk controlled" and "100% fully automated." AlgoTrades says their "proprietary INNER-Market Analysis method uses a number of data points including up/down volume flow, market sentiment, cycles, moving averages, volatility, momentum and price patterns which are recalculated on every tick." They utilize your own brokerage account to do the trading, but it must be from a list of their recommended brokers. They require a minimum of $35,000 to open an account (others require less), with a $300,000 maximum. They only trade the S&P 500 index using three mini futures contracts. The fees range from $1,500 to $4,000 a year, depending on what you go with. Naturally in the disclosure they say, "No representation is being made that utilizing the First Algorithmic Trading System will result in profitable trading or be free of risk of loss. Futures trading and trading exchange traded funds involve a substantial risk of loss and is not appropriate for everyone." In other words, there are no guarantees. I think you will find a better way in this book without the expensive fees they charge to profit in up and down markets.[24]

You can also fool around with ChatGPT and try and trade the market based on what you are able to get it to do for you, and you may do better than mutual fund managers, meaning you might beat the index, but this area isn't for most investors as there are many solutions they can provide for a trading strategy and you just don't know what will work. What you will read later in this book though works.

Shorting the Market

Most advisors do not recommend shorting the market because of their mantra of "buy and hold," and the assumption that stocks always go up. Also, if they are ever sued by an investor they advised to short an investment, they would more than likely lose the case and be reprimanded by the SEC for violating the Prudent Man Rule, which

---

[24] What I have done with my own company is create software that has my trading rules built into it, and that includes stops, trailing stops, taking profit on half shares and more. The key of course is picking the right entries, and you'll find out how to do that in the Trading Strategies chapter.

asks what a prudent man would do with his investments (hint: It's not "short the stock market"). Naturally, I disagree with the SEC on this. You can profit from shortening the market quite easily when stocks or ETFs are overbought.

It used to be that a stock had to tick higher to short it. If a stock was falling you could not just jump in short and ride it down. Today, however, you can buy inverse ETFs in almost any sector, whether it be the market indices, commodities, specific countries and more, and you do not need any uptick in the investment to trade this. But today, shorting stocks like Tesla (TSLA) for example can be done just by putting in a market or limit sell order at a specific price.

Many do not choose to short stocks or buy inverse ETFs because they are not familiar with the process, but the returns can be phenomenal when a sector turns south. You can also profit when turmoil from wars, Covid type scenarios of unknown viruses, or other calamities hit the economy.

The point here is for the investor to not be intimidated with articles that come out against shorting or timing the market. The rules have changed in favor of timing the market if you have the right tools to do so. Conversely, your financial advisor only trades one way typically, long the market.

Tax Planning - Taking Losses
(With non-IRA/401(k)/Pension Assets)

Too often, investors hold on to losing positions in their investments without taking advantage of the tax laws that can allow them to write off that loss against any gains in the year of the loss, and potentially subsequent years. This loss can be utilized against any capital gains for that year should you sell an investment that has capital appreciation, dollar for dollar, or the loss can be taken as a deduction from income earned up to $3,000 per year until it is exhausted in any subsequent years' capital gains or earned income. Please discuss with your accountant and take those losses if you have them.

There is one thing to watch out for: The "wash rule" states that you won't be allowed to buy the same asset back for 30 days, or you lose the exemptions—30 days is not long to wait, and chances are, whatever asset you sold for a loss is probably down more. Unfortunately, you do not get this tax loss capture benefit for your IRA/401(k)/pension investments. Also, if you are a full-time trader, you need to talk to your accountant to take the election before the tax year so you won't be subject to mark to market trades. It is a complicated area, but you cannot trade that stock for 30 days after buying it normally but as a professional trader, you are allowed to do so but you must make that election prior to your trading year beginning April 15th each year.

Review the Internal Revenue Code on trading at the link below and speak with your CPA about how to qualify. Here is what the IRS looks for.

- You must seek to profit from daily market movements in the prices of securities and not from dividends, interest, or capital appreciation.
- Your activity must be substantial; and
- You must carry on the activity with continuity and regularity.

The following facts and circumstances should be considered in determining if your activity is a securities trading business:

- Typical holding periods for securities bought and sold.
- The frequency and dollar amount of your trades during the year.
- The extent to which you pursue the activity to produce income for a livelihood; and
- The amount of time you devote to the activity.[25]

There is a way to sell your highly appreciated investments, whether real estate, stock, or even precious metals without paying tax on capital gains. It involves utilizing charitable trusts. Check with your tax advisor or contact someone at the Planned Giving Design Center and discover the many ways to use these trusts to eliminate tax on the capital gain when you sell appreciated assets while receiving some income tax benefits. http://www.pgdc.com/

At one point in my life I was a Certified Specialist in Planned Giving (CSPG) and these types of strategies are there for your

---

[25] https://www.irs.gov/taxtopics/tc429

utilization in investment and tax planning.[26] This is especially true for the highly appreciated real estate discussed in a later chapter.

Trading Economic Data and News

These two areas are mostly used by day traders but access to a news feed and knowing what daily economic data is coming out is necessary for a successful investor if you want to get in on trades that move with the market. When news comes out that can move a stock higher or lower, you can pay the expense of a Bloomberg terminal to be the first to know or rely on social media to get the news fast. This includes StockTwits, where you can share ideas with six million other investors or X which seems to provide information quickly. The most popular source for news though is CNBC, Fox Business and Bloomberg TV albeit slower for real time market moves. This media is more for swing traders or investors.

Some other sources for active traders are TradingView[27] and NextCapital,[28] which track all your investments in one place. A good analysis of the various social trading networks and platforms can be found at the footnote to this sentence.[29] TradingView offers a free peak before signing up for their service.

Check them out to see what fits your investment goals, objectives, and trading style. What you will find is a trading plan is still needed.

For trading economic data, go to the Economic Calendar at investing.com and you will be able to see data come in after just a few seconds' delay, typically at 8:30am Eastern time. [30] You will find this link and the important economic data that is forthcoming on the Profit in Up and Down Markets.

---

26 https://www.csulb.edu/research-foundation/american-institute-for-philanthropic-studies
27 https://www.tradingview.com/
28 https://nextcapital.com/#/
29 http://socialtradingguru.com/networks/social-trading-networks
30 https://www.investing.com/economic-calendar/

Chapter 5 - Investment Strategies to Consider

Philosophies on Investing

Sometimes when it comes to investing, you must simply use your brain and ask questions. What is the hottest trend? Who makes the products related to that trend? Where are we with the Baby Boomers? What will they be doing in retirement? Those who have money will spend it and you can invest accordingly.

Some of the industries that I see worth investing in for the coming years are those that either do well in tough times or have an upward growth that never seems to run out of customers, meaning the demand is always there. The following list of industries should be considered for a diversified portfolio.

Food-related, especially organic, as more people become health conscious.

Addiction/Enjoyment related industries – Alcohol, including spirits/wine/beer and coffee.

Entertainment/Hollywood - An escape mechanism.

Marijuana/Medicinal - Another escape mechanism and growth opportunity in some states and national approval.

Gambling/Online Gaming – People looking for ways to get ahead that only make the casinos rich.

Vitamins - Another growth industry for a health-conscious population.

Self-Driving Cars – Becoming more of a reality.

Robotics - The rise of machines is upon us whether it is to take your order at McDonalds or be a surgical assistant for one's operation. Tesla's Optimus robot is going to be amazing!

Artificial Intelligence (AI) this of course is a double-edged sword. Eliminating humans via the use of computers and machines for problem solving and decision making can be great for corporations but where will the jobs to provide you income come from?[31] You will have to be ahead of the game for your own employment to make sure you are not replaced and at the same time find the investment opportunities that will explode in the coming years. But in this arena, the stand out has been Nvidia (NVDA). Apple has also entered into the AI arena.[32]

Apple, Amazon, Alphabet (Google) and META(Facebook) along with Microsoft and Nvidia, are all powerhouses to contend with. Industries associated with any of these companies can do well. But keep an eye out for the next powerhouse to emerge by seeing what modern technology evolves. Of this group, I do not see a replacement for most of them but Amazon is one of those stocks that will always be a buy the dip scenario. As these companies go, collectively, so goes the market. Information technology makes up 29.2% of the S&P 500.

Asset Allocation

Diversification/Investment Pyramid

Your typical financial advisor views investing based on a pyramid of risk like the one in the next chart:[33] It is what I was taught three decades ago as a new financial advisor and has been adjusted to today's lingo with the introduction of derivatives.

31

https://www.uc.edu/content/dam/uc/ce/docs/OLLI/Page%20Content/ARTIFICI AL%20INTELLIGENCEr.pdf

[32] https://apnews.com/article/apple-artificial-intelligence-siri-iphone-software-conference-4217d67977f95ead880835a71ecce098

[33] http://srsinc.com/wp-content/uploads/PDF/Investment%20 Pyramid.pdf

Investment Pyramid

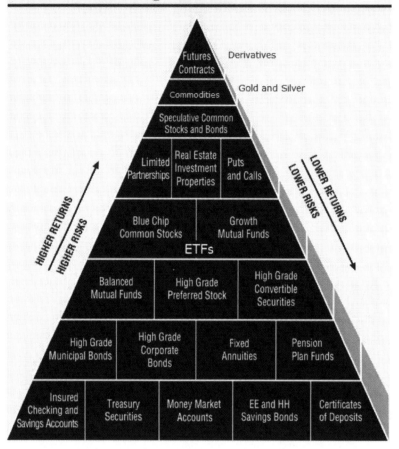

How did this pyramid hold up during the 2007–2009 fiscal crisis? Overall, every asset listed got hurt except the bottom row and some in the second to bottom row. But since that crisis we have seen every asset rise in value except for commodities which did not start rising again with some momentum until 2019. By 2024 gold is at all-time highs and ready for lift off once everyone realizes the Federal Reserve is, while still respected by Wall Street, always behind what is really going on. Silver is lagging and should outpace gold over the next few years. And if there is another crisis, it will be a monetary one led by even more banks going under. When Silicon Valley bank and a few others failed (and bailed out again) in 2023, gold and silver took off to the upside. The next move up for metals will be a big one.

Age-Appropriate Investing

An old adage says to put the percentage of your assets in stocks that inversely correlate to your age and the rest in bonds. If you are twenty, then 80% should go into stocks because you have more time to ride out the ups and downs of the stock market, and 20% would go into bonds. If you are eighty, then 20% should go into stocks as you have less time to recoup losses, and 80% into bonds. How did this philosophy work from 2007–2009? It did not. Losing 40-50% of your suggested allocation using this strategy is a big drawdown, especially if you are at or near retirement.

I really cannot get behind this strategy because you need stock exposure to provide your portfolio with some growth over time and many will need the dividend income some stocks provide. At age 80 you could miss out on easy profit because some silly rule tells you that your investments should be allocated a certain way—without knowing what is going on in the economy. For example, at ages 70 and 80 you would have missed the entire bull market with 70%/80% of your portfolio while in bonds from 2009 to 2021, and 2023 and 2024 (thus far to May) when stocks outperformed all other assets. When the Fed changed course and started raising interest rates, how did that affect this 70%/80% in bonds advice? It was not good for seniors, was it? From May to August 2024 however, bonds were performing well. When do you know what to be in? Hopefully you know the answer after reading this book and can be on the right side of the trend, up or down, stocks or bonds. However, the next crisis could take both stocks and bonds down with it depending on interest rates. Having an option to profit if they go lower is an important issue to resolve for your portfolio.

The best way to take the guessing game out of investing is to simply diversify your investments among asset classes and continually take from what is doing well or hitting new highs and allocate more to what is beaten down. But do not just do this automatically. You still must do some analysis and have a plan. Read on.

Not Every Trade Is a Winner

You must first know that you are not going to time investments. Not every trade will be a winner. You can come close though, if you have a system in place that allows you to sell near the top and buy near the bottom. There are techniques for this whether a short term or long term investor.

To know when to switch from one investment class to another, or out of stocks and into cash, open your eyes to what is going on—do a little reading. But do not just listen to the always bullish CNBC or the always bearish Zerohedge.com for what is going on in the markets. Use some of your own intuition and common sense about the markets. Ask yourself the following questions:

1. What does my financial advisor say to do? (They are almost always bullish on the market.)
2. Trade with the trend, not against it, unless you are allocating to a beaten-down sector with a proven strategy.
3. What do the charts say? Are you at support or resistance?
4. What are interest rates doing? If they are falling, be in bonds and bond funds. If they are rising, bond mutual funds are not the place to be. The Fed is ready to lower rates as they have let rates move too high as of August 2024 with the unemployment rate rising to 4.2%. Depending on when you read this book, know things may have changed, naturally, but the Fed isn't going to get rates back down to their 2% goal.
5. What is the VIX showing? The VIX shows 30-day market expectations of market volatility. Where is volatility? Are the markets calm and the VIX falling, or are the markets falling as the VIX rises? [34]

---

[34] http://vixcentral.com/historical?days=30

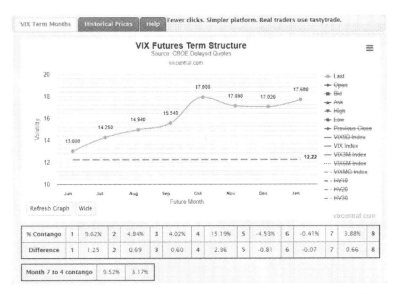

If VIX trending higher for future months, potential trouble ahead for markets. If trending lower, calmer waters ahead for markets. The VIX may be in Contango or Backwardation.

What Is Contango? Contango is a situation where the futures price of a commodity is higher than the spot price. You can see the first chart is pushing higher over the next several months. If an upward sloping curve, we have contango and longer term contracts are more expensive than shorter term contracts. There is an election coming up and lots of uncertainty. But also threats of war and an overpriced stock market.

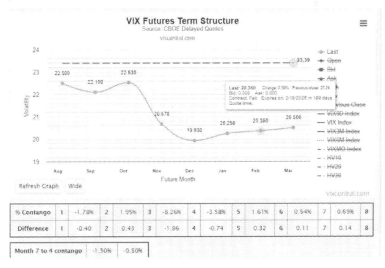

Backwardation is when the current price of an underlying asset is higher than prices trading in the futures market. If we have a downward sloping curve, it indicates that longer term contracts are cheaper than near term contracts as represented by the second chart.

6. What is the unemployment rate doing? If it is falling, stocks are great. If it is rising, one should be cautious with stocks. It is August of 2024 and the unemployment rate measured by U7 has been steadily rising and one should be cautious with stocks moving forward, taking profits on spikes.

7. Where are we with stocks' earnings per share compared to historic norm? Right now, we are above the mean based on the Shiller P/E Ratio.[35]

8. Is your neighbor telling you to buy this or that investment? If so, investigate trading in the opposite direction. As Warren Buffett has advised, be fearful when others are greedy and greedy when others are fearful. Buffet's fund, Berkshire Hathaway is presently $276.9 billion in cash up from $188 billion in May and before the last market decline that begin in July. What does he see? Nothing worth investing in is the current answer.

9. What is the Fed doing? Follow them but be aware at some point their game may fail (see gold section).

10. Predict the future. Open your eyes. Read. Become your own guru.

11. Know what is going on with inflation. The 1960s saw the Dow drop 35% during that inflationary episode. The 1970s had a two-year drop in 'seventy-three and 'seventy-four. Volcker and the Fed Chair's preceding him were tightening monetary policy in the late 'seventies and this did not help the markets, but loosening things up finally got the roaring 'eighties underway. The Fed is burying itself in its own balance sheet these days, so the reality is, they are clueless. More on that later.

---

[35] http://www.multpl.com/shiller-pe/

Sector Rotation

One of the secrets to trading various sectors is to look for the top companies in each sector and trade them.

Asset Allocation

Fitting right in with Asset Allocation is the Callan Periodic Table of Investment Returns.[36] The next tables show the annual returns from 1996–2015 of key indices ranked by performance. Please note that in 2008, it did not matter what you invested in, it did not do well. This is followed by an updated table through 2023.

The tables provide an indication of what is doing well and to add positions if they are breaking out., As the prices move higher you can add trailing stops as nothing goes straight up as you can see. Eventually there are reversals (buy low sell high).

Trailing stops are when you set a dollar or percentage exit price below the current price that will trigger if the price falls by that dollar amount or percentage. It is the amount you want to risk on any new trades or once in profit the amount you are willing to give back of your profit.

This for me is a smarter, more proactive way to diversify, among various sectors (more on sectors in a bit).

---

[36] https://www.callan.com/periodic-table/

The Callan Periodic Table of Investment Returns

Annual Returns for Key Indices Ranked in Order of Performance (2004–2023)

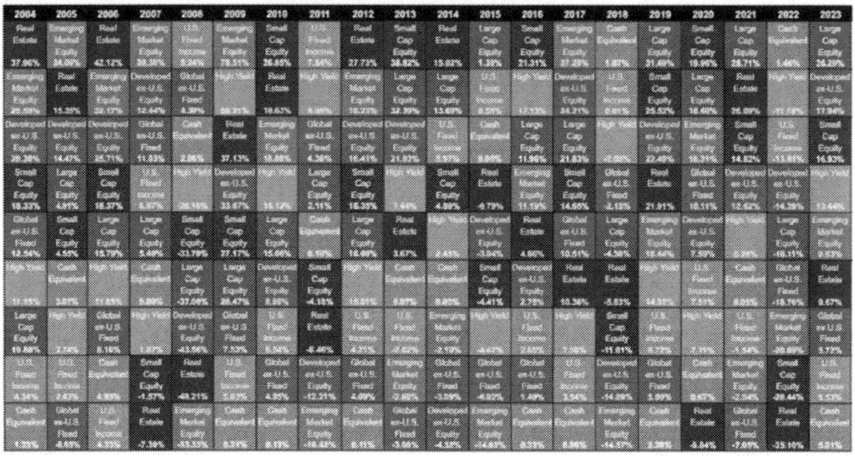

2004	2005	2006	2007	2008	2009	2010	2011	2012	2013	2014	2015	2016	2017	2018	2019	2020	2021	2022	2023

(Table data not legibly reproducible)

Blackrock Investments offers a different version of various sectors' performance over the years.

2014	2015	2016	2017	2018	2019	2020	2021	2022	2023	Annualised
REITs 22.8%	Japan equities 9.9%	High yield 14.3%	China equities 54.3%	Cash 1.9%	US equities 31.6%	China equities 29.7%	Commodities 38.5%	Commodities 22%	US equities 10.9%	US equities 11.1%
US equities 13.4%	US equities 1.3%	Infrastructure 12.4%	EM equities 37.8%	DM gov debt -0.4%	Infrastructure 27%	US equities 21.4%	REITs 32.5%	Cash 1.3%	Japan equities 6.6%	Infrastructure 6.4%
Infrastructure 13%	Emerging debt 1.2%	US equities 11.6%	Europe equities 26.2%	IG credit -3.5%	Europe equities 24.6%	EM equities 18.7%	US equities 27%	Infrastructure -0.2%	Commodities 5.7%	Japan equities 4.3%
China equities 8.3%	REITs 0.6%	EM equities 11.6%	Japan equities 24.4%	High yield -4.1%	REITs 24.5%	Japan equities 14.9%	Europe equities 17%	High yield -12.7%	Europe equities 4.6%	Europe equities 3.6%
Emerging debt 5.5%	Cash 0.1%	Emerging debt 10.2%	US equities 21.9%	US equities -4.5%	China equities 23.7%	IG credit 10.1%	Infrastructure 11.9%	Europe equities -14.5%	Cash 4.1%	REITs 3.3%
IG credit 2.5%	Europe equities -2.3%	Commodities 9.7%	Infrastructure 20.1%	Emerging debt -4.8%	Japan equities 20.1%	DM gov debt 9.5%	Japan equities 2%	IG credit -16.1%	High yield 4%	High yield 2.8%
Cash 0.1%	High yield -2.7%	IG credit 6.9%	High yield 10.4%	REITs -4.9%	EM equities 18.9%	High yield 7%	High yield 1%	Japan equities -16.3%	IG credit 0.1%	Emerging debt 1.8%
High yield 0%	DM gov debt -3.3%	IG credit 6%	Emerging debt 9.3%	Infrastructure -5.5%	Emerging debt 14.4%	Europe equities 5.9%	Cash 0%	Emerging debt -16.5%	Emerging debt -0.4%	EM equities 1.6%
DM gov debt -0.8%	IG credit -3.8%	Japan equities 2.7%	IG credit 9.3%	Commodities -10.7%	High yield 12.6%	Emerging debt 5.8%	Emerging debt -1.5%	DM gov debt -17.5%	EM equities -1.8%	Commodities 1.4%
EM equities -1.8%	China equities -7.6%	DM gov debt 1.7%	REITs 8.6%	Japan equities -12.6%	IG credit 11.6%	Cash 0.7%	IG credit -2.1%	US equities -19.5%	DM gov debt -4.9%	Cash 1.2%
Japan equities -3.7%	Infrastructure -11.5%	China equities 1.1%	DM gov debt 7.9%	EM equities -14.2%	Commodities 11.8%	Infrastructure -5.8%	EM equities -2.2%	EM equities -19.7%	Infrastructure -6.6%	China equities 1.2%
Europe equities -5.7%	EM equities -14.6%	Cash 0.4%	Commodities 1.7%	Europe equities -14.3%	DM gov debt 5.6%	REITs -8.1%	DM gov debt -6.6%	China equities -21.8%	REITs -8.1%	IG credit 1.1%
Commodities -17.9%	Commodities -23.4%	Europe equities 0.2%	Cash 0.8%	China equities -18.7%	Cash 2.3%	Commodities -9.3%	China equities -21.6%	REITs -23.8%	China equities -11.1%	DM gov debt -1.4%

Key: Equities   Bonds   Private markets, commodities

Past performance is not a reliable indicator of current or future results. It is not possible to invest directly in an index.
Sources: BlackRock Investment Institute, with data from LSEG Datastream, 3 November 2023

Getting More Specific with Sector Rotation

By spreading your risk among ETFs that represent multiple sectors, you are not putting your eggs in one basket. These ETFs allow you to go long or short a certain sector. You can trade with the trend.

The trend can change on a dime because of events or news and if we have gone one way too far, then you will need to time your exit strategy. The footnote following this sentence is kept up to date for the current hot and cold sectors and should be viewed daily by traders to look for trend reversals higher or lower. [37]

Communication Services and Technology have had a momentous year. Utilities, Energy, Health Care and Consumer Staples had a down year but all of those turned positive in the last few months when you could have bought low. How do you know what to do next? What kind of plan do you have? Buy and hold like your broker suggests has worked for decades. I understand this. Why not always stick with the trend though with a buy and sell strategy?

The following are results from November Year to Date (YTD) for the first sector tracker and through May 14, 2024, YTD for the second sector tracker.

SECTOR TRACKER

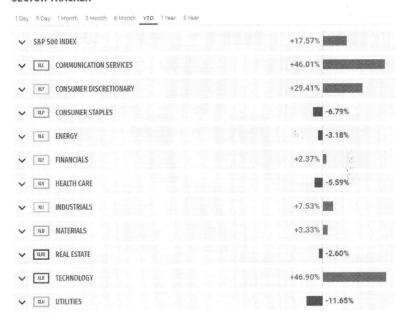

| 1 Day | 5 Day | 1 Month | 3 Month | 6 Month | YTD | 1 Year | 5 Year |

˅	S&P 500 INDEX	+17.57%
˅ XLC	COMMUNICATION SERVICES	+46.01%
˅ XLY	CONSUMER DISCRETIONARY	+29.41%
˅ XLP	CONSUMER STAPLES	-6.79%
˅ XLE	ENERGY	-3.18%
˅ XLF	FINANCIALS	+2.37%
˅ XLV	HEALTH CARE	-5.59%
˅ XLI	INDUSTRIALS	+7.53%
˅ XLB	MATERIALS	+3.33%
˅ XLRE	REAL ESTATE	-2.60%
˅ XLK	TECHNOLOGY	+46.90%
˅ XLU	UTILITIES	-11.65%

---

[37] https://www.sectorspdrs.com/sectortracker

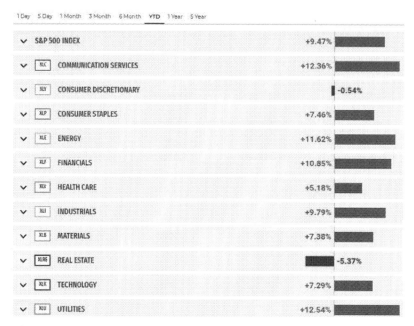

⌄		S&P 500 INDEX	+9.47%
⌄	XLC	COMMUNICATION SERVICES	+12.36%
⌄	XLY	CONSUMER DISCRETIONARY	-0.54%
⌄	XLP	CONSUMER STAPLES	+7.46%
⌄	XLE	ENERGY	+11.62%
⌄	XLF	FINANCIALS	+10.85%
⌄	XLV	HEALTH CARE	+5.18%
⌄	XLI	INDUSTRIALS	+9.79%
⌄	XLB	MATERIALS	+7.38%
⌄	XLRE	REAL ESTATE	-5.37%
⌄	XLK	TECHNOLOGY	+7.29%
⌄	XLU	UTILITIES	+12.54%

Technology has led the way and there are those out there that speculate central bank buying of just a few tech stocks has kept this market bull going. Buy the dip has worked for quite a while with this market. Bears have been in hibernation for about a decade. Recall what occurs about every 9 years or so; a recession. Technology can get hit hard when we slip into a recession, but most everything will be hit hard and cash becomes a viable alternative to park your funds, unless you understand that profit can be made on the downside too. Most investors do not realize this as they are programmed with their 401ks to only have choices that go up with the markets. Inverse ETFs are never offered by the plan administrators who give you choices of investments for your 401k. Why is that? Think about that long and hard.

Market Valuations

One way to see whether today's stock market is undervalued or overvalued is to compare the market cap to GDP. According to Gurufocus, the ratio of market cap to GDP is at 185.50 as of 5/12/24, well above the pre-2007-2009 crisis high of 110.70. This is another signal of a market potentially topping soon.[38] As a trader/investor, I do not care if it shows we are overvalued presently or not. If I am still long the market, I will ride it if it lets me, but I will keep an eye on the other side and look for signs to jump short.

From the gurufocus website:

"As of 2024-05-14 03:20:00 PM CDT (updates daily): The Stock Market is Significantly Overvalued according to Buffett Indicator. Based on the historical ratio of total market cap over GDP (currently at 186.5%), it is likely to return 0.5% a year from this level of valuation, including dividends. Meanwhile, based on the historical ratio of newly introduced total market cap over GDP plus Total Asset of Federal Reserve Banks (currently at 147.8%), the stock market is Significantly Overvalued, and it is likely to return 1% a year from this level of valuation, including dividends."

But keep in mind, they also said it was significantly overvalued in November of 2023.

Over the long run, stock market valuation reverts to its mean. A higher current valuation certainly correlates with lower long-term returns in the future. On the other hand, a lower current valuation level correlates with a higher long-term return. The total market valuation is measured by the ratio of total market cap (TMC) to GNP -- the equation representing Warren Buffett's "best single measure". This ratio since 1970 is shown in the second chart to the right. Gurufocus.com calculates and updates this ratio daily. As of 11/18/2023, this ratio is 163.7%.

We can see that, during the past five decades, the TMC/GNP ratio has varied within a very wide range. Based on current value and historical month-end values, the lowest point was about 32.7% in the previous deep recession in July 1982, while the highest point was about 199.5% in August 2021. The market went from Significantly undervalued in July 1982 to Significantly overvalued in August 2021.

Based on these historical valuations, we have divided market valuation into five zones:

Ratio = Total Market Cap / GDP	Valuation
Ratio ≤ 81%	Significantly Undervalued
81% < Ratio ≤ 104%	Modestly Undervalued
104% < Ratio ≤ 127%	Fair Valued
127% < Ratio ≤ 150%	Modestly Overvalued
Ratio > 150%	Significantly Overvalued
Where are we today (2023-11-18)?	Ratio = 163.7%. **Significantly Overvalued**

Special Note on When a Bear Market Takes Hold

You'll see later in this book an analysis of what is called a heat map of the market, showing in colors what the overall trend is. If red, it's not good for stocks and if green it's good. At the end of July to the beginning of August we had the market begin to turn south. My

---

[38] http://www.gurufocus.com/stock-market-valuations.php

trading service was providing trades and all of them were short signals during this time. I listen to the data not what someone on X says to do. My data always tells the truth.

There is a website finwiz that provides financial visualizations or this heat map I speak of. You can see their work in the following charts. There was a huge down day in the market on August 2nd, 2024 for the U.S.markets. Why? The market had already started to decline per the data and trades I was seeing coming in. There was the ongoing threat of war between Israel and its surrounding neighbors and the threat of Iran stepping in and escalating things with rumors of Russia, who is already involved in a war with Ukraine, sending over to Iran military support. You'll see in the next chapter you would have been in certain stocks during this time of uncertainty but we also had an overbought stock market.

The following snapshot is of all sectors and for the most part no sector was left unscathed except for some health/medical and household/beverages.

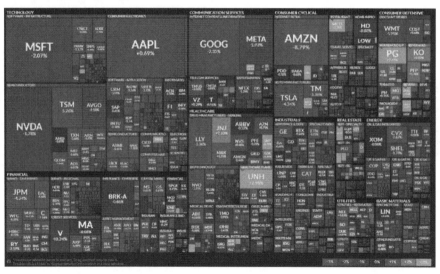

The S&P 500 Index which millions are invested in through their Index Funds got hit pretty hard too.

It wasn't just the U.S. markets that got hit but all world markets were hit. This is why it's important to look at all the signals to see if your investments line up with what's going on.

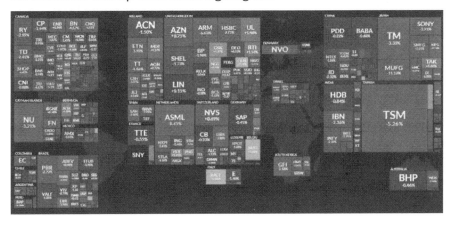

CHAPTER 6 - INVESTMENT CATEGORIES TO CONSIDER (HOW TO THINK OUTSIDE THE BOX)

Where Do Your Tax Dollars Go? Can you profit from this insider knowledge?

There are certain industries that benefit from how the government spends your tax dollars. It makes sense, then, as part of your investment philosophy, to invest in these industries. Why? Because you know they will be funded by the government. Sometimes it is even mandated that they be funded.

In 2015 there were $428,950,903,231 in federal outlays to more than 3.6 million companies. There was also $614,050,292,215 in grants handed out. That is over $1 trillion of your tax dollars that you can follow to the recipient—and profit from, with a little bit of digging.

The largest benefactors of this government spending, making up 49% of the outlay, are the defense and healthcare industries, as outlined in the next graphic.[39] The 2019 budget is the same amount budgeted for Defense and Healthcare spending as 2016. A slightly higher percentage though in Welfare and Interest with the Fed's move to raise rates. In 2019 you can see from the next chart that the government outflow was projected to be $350 billion for the next 5 years, mostly for healthcare and defense.

| Estimated Outlays in $ billion nominal -5yr -1yr as of Winter 2019 | | | | | | |
Change View: people old *functions* radical census programs altprog oldprog COFOG	FY 2019 Outlays	FY 2020 Outlays	FY 2021 Outlays	FY 2022 Outlays	FY 2023 Outlays	FY 2024 Outlays
[+] Health Care	1,252.2	1,301.2	1,371.4	1,442.7	1,481.6	1,512.8
[+] Defense	939.4	1,008.5	1,046.5	1,072.6	1,076.0	1,079.8

---

[39] http://www.usgovernmentspending.com/federal_budget

FY20 Federal Budget Pie Chart

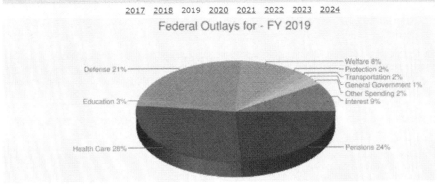

2017 2018 2019 2020 2021 2022 2023 2024

Federal Outlays for - FY 2019

Defense 21%
Education 3%
Health Care 28%
Welfare 8%
Protection 2%
Transportation 2%
General Government 1%
Other Spending 2%
Interest 9%
Pensions 24%

In 2024 you can bet with all the military spending the government is doing for Ukraine and Israel, projections are meaningless. When you have an unlimited checkbook fueled by a willing and able Federal Reserve to fund the spending, is it any wonder that every time Congress votes on the debt ceiling, they raise it?

Projections through the year 2034 have interest on the debt going from 9% in 2019 to 21% by 2024 and Social Security jumping to 28%.

Health Care, Social Security, and Interest Explain 84% of Projected Spending Growth

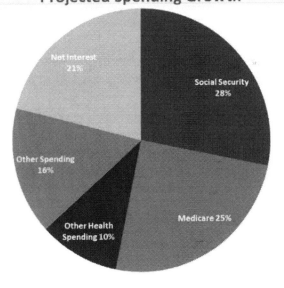

Net Interest 21%
Social Security 28%
Other Spending 16%
Medicare 25%
Other Health Spending 10%

CRFB.org

ce: Congressional Budget Office

Defense Spending

If the government is looking for action militarily, which is something it does quite often no matter who is in control of Congress or the Presidency, Democrats or Republicans, then an investor can profit from these activities by investing in companies that represent the military industrial complex. I mentioned this strategy in my Illusions of Wealth book written in 2016. C. Companies like Lockheed Martin, Boeing, General Dynamics, and Raytheon.

Lockheed received over $50 million in 2022, Raytheon over $27 million and General Dynamics over $25 million with Boeing coming in at $17 million. [40]

For 2023 Lockheed received contracts worth $68.5 billion. Raytheon $27.8 million. Boeing $14.8 million. General Dynamics $22.9 million. Northrop Grumman $15[41]

You can see this graphically by looking historically at this defense industry relationship with the US government. In 2015 you can see by the graph below that when the war machine escalates, so does the government funding. What has been happening lately in the U.S. is involvement in Ukraine and Israel and threat of escalation with China over Taiwan.

Contracts Recorded: 2,874
Contracts Value: $334,706,539,721

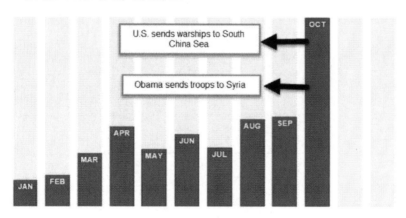

---

[40] https://thehill.com/homenews/4110571-government-paid-companies-most-money-in-2022/

[41] https://news.clearancejobs.com/2024/03/12/top-10-u-s-defense-contractors-report-has-lockheed-martin-leading-fy23/

How does this spending by the government help the defense industry? Below you can see how Lockheed Martin, with all its government contracts, has easily beat the returns of the S&P 500 Index. Please also note that the industry in general has outperformed the S&P 500 Index.

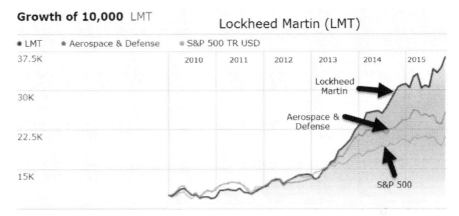

If we look at 2019, we can see nothing has really changed with the performance of Lockeed Martin (LMT). The adage: follow the money, comes into mind here. You do not have to reinvent the wheel when it comes to investing. You just need to follow where government money is going and tag along.

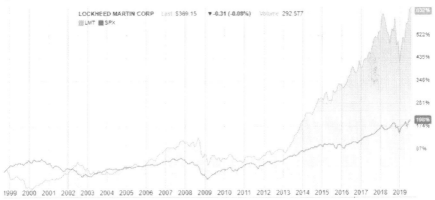

In November 2023, Lockheed Martin Corporation was sitting at $444 a share over double where it was in 2015. May of 2024 and Lockheed is at $467.18. Knowing how our government works helps. Corporations control Congress and get contracts for their war machine, and you can benefit from this insight. When we looked at the heat map you just read about and the carnage on Aug 2nd that occurred, Lockheed, which was trading up to 548 was down -0.02%. It held up well.

You can view all the contracts awarded to the U.S. Department of Defense each day at the defense.gov website.[42] Invest accordingly based on all you learn in this book. The footnote to this sentence you'll find the link to see where government money goes.[43] It just could be your key to successful investing.

Healthcare Spending

Before Covid even hit, drug companies were benefiting from special relationships with corporations, receiving contracts from the government. Add to that health care subsidies and these industries were two of the biggest vendors receiving contracts from the government each year, only surpassed by National Defense spending.

Merck and Pfizer have historically been the top two recipients of these government contracts, and since 2010 we have seen their stocks perform quite well, with Pfizer readily beating the S&P 500. Pfizer scored $18 billion in contracts and went from $1 billion in contracts before the Covid-19 pandemic to over $14.1 billion in 2021. You can see that healthcare spending has not stopped. Moderna was a stock darling to jump on board during Covid 19, going from $29 a share to over $400. It fell to $76 a share in November of 2023 and bounced to $128 May of 2024 only to fall to 86.58 by August. Yes, you could have played both sides of that trade, long and short but you need to know what side to be on. Waiting for the right signals helps.

You will find the current award distributions with the link footnoted here.[44]

Socially Responsible Investing

From Google AI - ESG investing focuses on companies that follow positive environmental, social, and governance principles. Investors are

---

[42] http://www.defense.gov/News/Contracts
[43] https://www.usaspending.gov/#/recipient
[44] https://www.usaspending.gov/#/download_center/award_data_archive

increasingly eager to align their portfolios with ESG-related companies and fund providers, making it an area of growth with positive effects on society and the environment.

You want to be able to follow trends that society feels strongly about and thus funnel money in that direction. Be aware of ESG funds that appear to capitalize on this.

Consumer Spending - Where Do Consumers Spend Money?

Another investment opportunity that offers investors a way to profit is learning where consumers spend their wealth. The government releases the consumer expenditures report once a year and the next table shows the top categories of consumer spending by year.[45]

It is also important to know whether that expenditure is rising or falling, based on current economic conditions. They are terribly slow with their data, but it is still valuable to see where money flows.[46] What follows is a synopsis of the change from 2014 through mid-2018 (new release of data is September 2019)[47]

As of 2023, it is the Food category that has increased with gasoline expenditures moving higher and apparel and vehicle purchases declining. The next two tables below show spending 2012-2014 vs 2016-2018 vs 2020-2022. As of May 2024, there is no data yet for 2023.

Follow the spending for your investment portfolio.

Item	2012	2013	2014	Percent change 2012-2013	Percent change 2013-2014
Average income before taxes	$65,596	$63,784	$66,877	-2.8	4.8
Average annual expenditures	$51,442	$51,100	$53,495	-0.7	4.7
Food	6,599	6,602	6,759	0.0	2.4
Food at home	3,921	3,977	3,971	1.4	-0.2
Food away from home	2,678	2,625	2,787	-2.0	6.2
Housing	16,887	17,148	17,798	1.5	3.8
Shelter	9,891	10,080	10,491	1.9	4.1
Owned dwellings	6,056	6,108	6,149	0.9	0.7
Rented dwellings	3,186	3,324	3,631	4.3	9.2
Apparel and services	1,736	1,604	1,786	-7.6	11.3
Transportation	8,998	9,004	9,073	0.1	0.8
Gasoline and motor oil	2,756	2,611	2,468	-5.3	-5.5
Vehicle insurance	1,018	1,013	1,112	-0.5	9.8
Healthcare	3,556	3,631	4,290	2.1	n/a
Health insurance	2,061	2,229	2,868	8.2	n/a
Entertainment	2,605	2,482	2,728	-4.7	9.9
Cash contributions	1,913	1,834	1,788	-4.1	-2.5
Personal insurance and pensions	5,591	5,528	5,726	-1.1	3.6
All other expenditures	3,557	3,267	3,548	-8.2	8.6

n/a - Because of the questionnaire change for health insurance, the 2013-14 percent change is not strictly comparable to prior years.

---

[45] http://www.bls.gov/news.release/pdf/cesan.pdf
[46] http://www.bls.gov/cex/
[47] https://www.bls.gov/news.release/pdf/cesmy.pdf

Item	July 2016-June 2017 Average	July 2017-June 2018 Average	Percent change July 2016 - June 2017 to July 2017 - June 2018
Income before taxes	$73,207	$76,335	4.3
Average annual expenditures	58,460	60,815	4.0
Food	7,407	7,869	6.2
Food at home	4,121	4,445	7.9
Food away from home	3,286	3,424	4.2
Housing	19,325	20,001	3.5
Apparel and services	1,771	1,850	4.5
Transportation	9,252	9,735	5.2
Healthcare	4,710	4,924	4.5
Entertainment	2,941	3,379	14.9
Education	1,372	1,505	9.7
Cash contributions	2,088	1,840	-11.9
Personal insurance and pensions	6,938	6,904	-0.5
Pensions and Social Security	6,554	6,474	-1.2
All other expenditures	2,655	2,808	5.8

Table A. Average income and expenditures of all consumer units, 2020-22

Item	2020	2021	2022	Percent change 2020-21	Percent change 2021-22
Number of consumer units (000's)	131,234	133,595	134,090	0.0	0.0
Average income before taxes	$84,352	$87,432	$94,003	3.7	7.5
Average annual expenditures	$61,332*	$66,928	$72,967	9.1	9.0
Food	7,310*	8,289	9,343	13.4	12.7
Food at home	4,935*	5,259	5,703	6.6	8.4
Food away from home	2,375	3,030	3,639	27.6	20.1
Alcoholic beverages	478	554	583	15.9	5.2
Housing	21,417*	22,624	24,298	5.6	7.4
Owned dwellings	7,473	7,591	8,230	1.6	8.4
Rented dwellings	4,408	4,684	4,990	6.3	6.5
Other lodging	722	983	1,287	36.1	30.9
Lodging on out-of-town trips	318	604	837	89.9	38.6
Apparel and services	1,434	1,754	1,945	22.3	10.9
Transportation	9,826	10,961	12,295	11.6	12.2
Vehicle purchases (net outlays)	4,523	4,828	4,496	6.7	-6.9
Gasoline, other fuels, and motor oil	1,568	2,148	3,120	37.0	45.3
Public and other transportation	263	452	845	71.9	86.9
Healthcare	5,177	5,452	5,850	5.3	7.3
Health insurance	3,667	3,704	3,843	1.0	3.8
Medical services	864	1,070	1,184	23.8	10.7
Entertainment	2,909*	3,568	3,458	22.7	-3.1
Fees and admissions	425	654	833	53.9	27.4
Pets toys, hobbies, and playground equipment	859	969	908	12.8	-6.3
Other entertainment supplies, equipment, and services	576*	925	698	60.6	-24.5
Personal care products and services	646	771	866	19.3	12.3
Reading	114	114	117	0.0	2.6
Education	1,271	1,226	1,335	-3.5	8.9
Tobacco products and smoking supplies	315	341	371	8.3	8.8
Miscellaneous	907	986	1,009	8.7	2.3
Cash contributions	2,283	2,415	2,755	5.8	14.1
Personal insurance and pensions	7,246	7,873	8,742	8.7	11.0
Pensions and Social Security	6,760	7,400	8,223	9.5	11.1

Chapter 7 - Most Popular Investment Alternatives

Index Funds

I am writing about index funds before mutual funds and doing so because this is where your money should be invested if you are the type of investor who prefers to go it alone and hold the biggest stocks and believe in the philosophy of buy and hold. The reason you invest in an index fund is you have access to the nation's largest corporations, and some may say the best because if you do not hold your weight in the index, you are kicked out of the index. The fees are low with index funds, and you do not need to pay a financial advisor any fees to invest in them.

Index funds are clearly a better choice for investors than managed mutual funds and most hedge funds, as we have pointed out the latter two consistently do not beat the market.

Investors have already woken up to the fact that index funds are a wonderful way to invest as the next chart shows. It is also a reason for the stocks in these indexes to keep rising. Demand from index investing alone is pushing some of these stocks to lofty levels and an index fund investor needs to know there is a tipping point and when investors exit because of weakness, their index fund will fall with the overall market.

Net new cash flow to index mutual funds in the United States from 2000 to 2022 (in billion U.S. dollars)

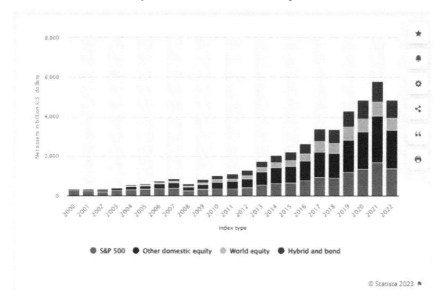

Investors plowed about $89 billion into US mutual funds and ETFs in March and the first quarter of 2024 ended with $189 billion of inflows according to Morningstar.[48]

Are There Warning Signs for Index Funds?

As increased money flows into the index funds though, investors in them are going to be in for a massive surprise collectively when the market shifts gear. This is where locking in profit and analyzing other strategies offered in this book can help you maintain your wealth if not grow it during a declining market.

Investors who take control of their investments can flip to shorting the market via inverse ETFs (discussed later) whereas an index fund, as great as they have been in a bull market, cannot protect you from any downside. The holder of an index fund will see their investments fall with the markets.

The same goes for most mutual fund holders as mutual fund managers' hands are tied to what the prospectus dictates, they invest in, which is going long the stock market except for a handful of inverse funds discussed later.

---

[48] https://www.morningstar.com/business/insights/blog/funds/us-fund-flows

In 2018 we saw the S&P lose -4.38% and index funds fell with it. In 2022 the same.

In 2000, 2001, 2002 we saw the S&P lose -9.1%, -11.89%, and -22.10%. That is a 40%+ decline. In 2008 there was a -37% decline. 1929 – 1932 saw 4 years straight of declines. Declines can happen. And yes, most will not have any power over their wealth to know when to get out and prevent those losses because of prevailing mentality. They stick with what their brokers have been taught, to buy and hold. I am here to tell you that you do not have to sit through a downturn and lose a chunk of your wealth. You can profit during downturns. Or if you have a 401k, know when to move to cash until the selling subsides.

There is no sin against profiting on a move south in the markets even when most of those around you will be losing money.

Dividend-Paying Stocks

One sign of a healthy company is when they are paying dividends to the investor. Dividends used to represent 60% of the total return for stock investments. We have heard for decades that stock returns average 10% over time, and while this was true, that 10% was divided as follows: 4% of the return was growth and 6% from a dividend for a 10% total.

Today we have an average 1.62% dividend yield for the S&P 500, down from 1.85% 4 years ago. This means if we were to average 10% total return, we would have to get 8.38% of that return from growth. But a dividend paying stock is better than one that is not paying dividends most of the time because it shows it is profitable enough for a company to do so.

According to Jim Atkinson from Guiness/Atkinson Asset Management Inc., there are five good reason to invest in quality dividend stocks:

1. Dividend stocks have historically outperformed overall.
2. Dividend stocks are less volatile.
3. Dividends can increase over time.
4. Historically, dividend growth has exceeded the rate of inflation.

5. Historically, companies that pay higher dividends and experience higher earnings growth.[49]

There are still some companies out there that continue to pay good dividends. There may be an opportunity for some of these dividend-paying companies to pay you an income that can keep pace with inflation. Yes, the Net Asset Value (NAV) may get hit on a market downturn, but income will be a difficult thing to come by in the years ahead, as you'll be limited to many asset classes that will be hurt by a market downturn like stocks, bonds and real estate (discussed later) or lag real current rates like annuity returns will do. In good times, dividend paying companies obviously are a wonderful way to invest.

The top ten dividend-paying companies as of 8/31/23 are below. This will change with time naturally. The top ten dividend-paying stocks as of May 2024 according to Morningstar are averaging about 4% now, much lower than what you see below. CDs at the bank are paying more than that in 2024 without market risk (only dollar risk or purchasing power risk discussed later).[50]

S&P 500 Highest dividend stocks and full list ranked by diviend yield (**USA 1.99% average**)

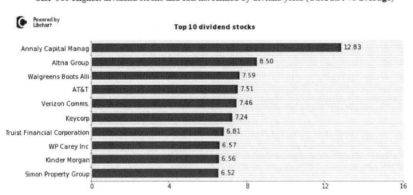

Mutual Funds

The amount invested in mutual funds has grown from $15.85 trillion in 2014 to $17.7 trillion by the end of 2018 and to $32.96 trillion by June of 2023. $8.2 trillion of that comes from IRA's and

---

[49] https://www.gafunds.com/wp-content/uploads/2018/08/Dividends-Matter-FINAL.pdf

[50] https://www.morningstar.com/stocks/10-best-dividend-stocks

401k type plans. The entire retirement market in the U.S. is 38.4 trillion as of 12/31/23 up 12.4% for the year. You can see that mutual funds are an important asset class for growing wealth. Exchange Traded Funds make up 3.4 trillion in 2019 and jumped to $8.12 trillion a 24.7% increase over 2022. The United States are the largest investors in mutual funds with Europe at $16.5 trillion, Asia-Pacific at $6.4 trillion and the rest of the world $2.7 trillion.

Asia has 4.5 billion people. Europe 738.8 million and the U.S. 329 million. 101.6 million in the U.S. own mutual funds representing 57.2 million households with an average balance of $150,000.

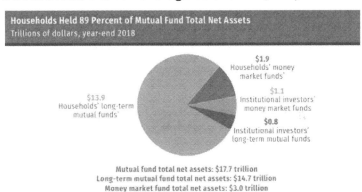

Households Held 89 Percent of Mutual Fund Total Net Assets
Trillions of dollars, year-end 2018

$1.9
Households' money market funds*

$1.1
Institutional investors' money market funds

$0.8
Institutional investors' long-term mutual funds

$13.9
Households' long-term mutual funds*

Mutual fund total net assets: $17.7 trillion
Long-term mutual fund total net assets: $14.7 trillion
Money market fund total net assets: $3.0 trillion

* Mutual funds held as investments in individual retirement accounts, defined contribution retirement plans, variable annuities, 529 plans, and Coverdell education savings accounts are counted as household holdings of mutual funds.

This data is derived from the 2019 Investment Company Fact Book.[51] By 2023, Total net mutual fund assets jumped to $22.1 trillion.

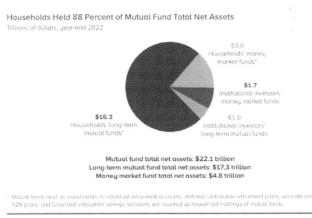

Households Held 88 Percent of Mutual Fund Total Net Assets
Trillions of dollars, year-end 2022

$3.0
Households' money market funds*

$1.7
Institutional investors' money market funds

$1.0
Institutional investors' long-term mutual funds

$16.3
Households' long-term mutual funds*

Mutual fund total net assets: $22.1 trillion
Long-term mutual fund total net assets: $17.3 trillion
Money market fund total net assets: $4.8 trillion

* Mutual funds held as investments in individual retirement accounts, defined contribution retirement plans, variable annuities, 529 plans, and Coverdell education savings accounts are counted as household holdings of mutual funds.

---

[51] https://www.ici.org/pdf/2019_factbook.pdf

Worldwide the U.S. markets are viewed as the safest and strongest where money will flow in times of global distress.

The key to investing in mutual funds, outside of the index funds, is to find managers who have been with the fund longer than three years and have a good track record of outperforming other funds in the same sector. Morningstar.com is a reliable source to compare funds against each other, and your financial advisor should be able to provide you with data sheets from them to analyze. Keep an eye on management changes too as when a good manager leaves the fund, it typically begins to perform poorly.[52]

We can see many investors taking their money out of mutual funds that do not simply follow the market and put them into index funds and in 2022 there was a massive outflow as the market headed south.

Net new cash flow to index mutual funds in the United States from 2000 to 2022 (in billion U.S. dollars)

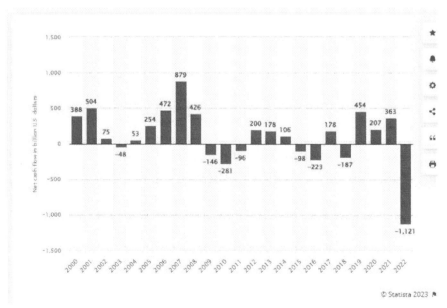

© Statista 2023

[52] https://www.moneyobserver.com/news/if-your-funds-star-manager-quits-your-returns-will-likely-be-lower

Increasingly advisors are moving clients to other alternative investments like ETFs as you see in the following chart (ETFs are discussed in detail later).

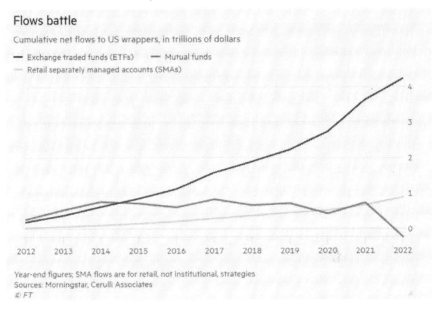

Flows battle

Cumulative net flows to US wrappers, in trillions of dollars

— Exchange traded funds (ETFs)   — Mutual funds
— Retail separately managed accounts (SMAs)

Year-end figures; SMA flows are for retail, not institutional, strategies
Sources: Morningstar, Cerulli Associates
© FT

As pointed out earlier, as of the end of 2023, ETFs have doubled in size in about 4 years.

Types of Mutual Funds

Many investors have 401k's and are limited to investing in mutual funds. You will still be able to use the Trading Strategies found in this book to manage your funds invested in your 401k. However, you will be limited as to your choices of investment until you either leave the company (retire, let go) and roll your 401k over into your self-directed IRA.

There are many diverse types of mutual funds that represent all aspects of the market, from large-cap to mid-cap to small-cap stocks, all the way down to bond funds for the more conservative investor. You can look at Morningstar and see what companies your fund invests in and see if you like it.

A mutual fund is good in the sense that it is diversified into more than one company, spreading the risk. If one company does bad, you have many more that can buoy the loss of the company that is underperforming.

You can also see which stocks the funds own by going to Yahoo Finance and putting in the mutual fund symbol and getting a lot of the data on the stocks it owns for free that might otherwise cost you to retrieve such data from Morningstar.

On the Yahoo Finance website, click on "Holders" after putting in the mutual fund or stock symbol you want to analyze and see what percentage of the stock is held by institutions as well as which funds are the biggest holders of the stock. You will also want to check out an important subcategory that is labeled "Insider Transactions" that will provide you with the ability to look and see if insiders are buying or selling their shares of a particular stock a fund owns. Selling of company stock by insiders would of course not be a good sign and buying of course a good sign.

On the Yahoo Finance page of a stock, you will find under "Statistics" and important data like the 50- and 200-day moving averages (discussed later), percentage of shares short and the 52-week high and low. Having a big picture of where the stock is provides you with timing strategies.

You can also find percentages of shares short in a stock. Many may be familiar with what Reddit and Wall Street Bets investors did with a stock called Game Stop (GME). Hedge funds were heavily short and one person, an average Joe investor Keith Gill got many others to what is called HODL (Hold on for Dear Life) the stock and force hedge funds, by massive buying of GME, to cover their shorts or take on huge losses.

These investors managed to bankrupt one of these hedge funds, Melvin Capital, who lost billions of dollars. Many of the investors like Keith Gill came out with huge profits when they finally sold their shares. They even made a movie about him called *Dumb Money*; a term prescribed to retail investors who normally do not win the stock trading game.

Game Stop (GME) just the last couple of months has moved up and down over 100% several times. Then in the middle of the night, Game Stop CEO diluted the shares of current stockholders by issuing more shares and warning about earnings. GME has seen the volume go down again since its revival as a meme stock. The average volume has been 53 million shares traded a day to 8.8 million on the Friday carnage day. When it comes to these types of meme stocks, I choose to stay away from them as one can get hurt pretty badly following their greedy tendencies.

Inverse Funds

Inverse funds have not been as popular in the last 10 years with the market zooming higher, but they are there for those who want to profit from an eventual bear market should we head into a recession. ProFunds short NASDAQ-100 Inv Fund (SOPIX) or the Rydex Inverse S&P 500 2X Inverse Strategy A Fund (RYTMX) are a couple of good ones.

These bear market funds can short certain asset classes or even countries. For example, if you wanted to short China, you could put some money in ProFunds UltraShort China Inv (UHPIX). Short Japan you will use the ProFunds UltraShort Japan Inv (UKPSX).

You can find a list of many more bear market funds and analyze their holdings and do the ratio analysis with these stocks they are shorting. Short the worst of them.

Morningstar.com has a list of bear funds. Every single bear fund shows negative returns for the one, 3 and 5 years.[53]

Bonds

Bonds represent $3.46 trillion of total mutual fund assets, and these funds are subject to interest rate risk. When interest rates begin to move higher, like they have mostly from 2021-2024, these mutual funds' NAV (Net Asset Value) will decline.

We have already addressed how bond diversification has not helped investors in the last few years. Apply what you have learned in this book before you invest in bonds.

Individual Bonds

Holders of individual bonds have a specified coupon rate and will fulfill that bond payment upon maturity. For me this is the best way to

---

[53] https://www.tradingsim.com/blog/learn-invest-bear-funds

invest in bonds as you know you will get the exact amount upon maturity, barring default of course.. Many high-income investors buy tax free bonds, but they too will lag rising interest rates. Bond mutual funds are not where you want to be in a rising interest rate environment. The quality of the bond is important as well. The lower the bond rating, the higher the return but the higher the risk of default.

Certificates of Deposit (CDs) and Money Market Funds

CDs and money market funds are places to keep liquid cash and for many years have not paid much interest. The rate of return will increase as rates rise with no real downside risk. Bankrate.com has a listing of the nation's top-paying CDs and money market funds.[54] For bank CDs, you can also use the site to compare the ratings of each financial institution and pick one you are comfortable with.[55]

I do like CDs as a very safe investment in retirement when interest rates are ticking higher. A.A laddered approach in buying CDs with varying length of maturities no longer than 3 years makes sense. Even one year to me is better as rates will rise quickly when the economy starts to sputter. If rates really start moving higher, you do not want to be stuck with a longer-term CD.

Presently there is a $250,000 FDIC backing for each individual bank account you maintain (this can be higher if structured correctly). For credit unions, the National Credit Union Administration (NCUA) is the independent agency that administers the National Credit Union Share Insurance Fund (NCUSIF) which also is $250,000.[56]

---

[54] http://www.bankrate.com/
[55] http://www.bankrate.com/funnel/savings/savings-results.aspx
[56] https://www.mycreditunion.gov/share-insurance

CHAPTER 8 - EXCHANGE-TRADED FUNDS (ETFs) AND EXCHANGE-TRADED NOTES (ETNs)

Now for some fun with investing!

ETFs are what I will talk about mostly in this chapter, and since their introduction they have brought about excitement in trading again as you can put your money into many different sectors of the market and could go both long and short that sector. But there can be a downside to leveraged ETFs you must be aware of. Let us start with a definition from Investopedia of what and ETF and ETN are first.

ETF - An exchange-traded fund (ETF) is a collection of securities—such as stocks—that tracks an underlying index. The best-known example is the SPDR S&P 500 ETF (SPY), which tracks the S&P 500 Index. ETFs can contain many types of investments, including stocks, commodities, bonds, or a mixture of investment types. An exchange-traded fund is a marketable security, meaning it has an associated price that allows it to be easily bought and sold.

ETN - Exchange-traded notes (ETNs) are types of unsecured debt securities that track an underlying index of securities and trade on a major exchange like a stock. ETNs are like bonds but do not pay interest payments. Instead, the prices of ETNs fluctuate like stocks.

ETFs and ETNs have become one of the most popular ways to invest, like index funds, because of their low fees and liquidity. Examples of where you can invest are stock indexes, bonds, commodities, industries, regions, countries, natural resources, currency, real estate, volatility, and even Bitcoin and other crypto currencies. Many of these you can leverage 2 to 3 times utilizing leveraged ETFs.

You can find a wonderful list of the ETFs that track certain sectors at the ETF Database site.[57] Click on each sector and it will reveal the multitude of ETFs you can trade both long and short. Remember to

---

[57] https://etfdb.com/etfs/

trade in the ones that have the most liquidity, which we will address shortly.

You can find at the end of this sentence a couple more good interactive ETF screeners.[58][59]

You can see the popularity of ETFs illustrated in the following two graphics.

Investment Company Total Net Assets by Type					
Billions of dollars, year-end					
	Mutual funds	Closed-end funds[1]	ETFs[2]	UITs	Total[3]
1999	6,834	157	34	92	7,116
2000	6,956	150	66	74	7,245
2001	6,969	145	83	49	7,246
2002	6,380	161	102	36	6,680
2003	7,399	216	151	36	7,801
2004	8,093	255	228	37	8,614
2005	8,889	276	301	41	9,507
2006	10,395	299	423	50	11,167
2007	11,995	316	608	53	12,973
2008	9,619	185	531	29	10,364
2009	11,109	224	777	38	12,149
2010	11,831	239	992	51	13,113
2011	11,630	244	1,048	60	12,982
2012	13,054	265	1,337	72	14,728
2013	15,049	282	1,675	87	17,092
2014	15,877	292	1,975	101	18,244
2015	15,658	263	2,101	94	18,116
2016	16,353	265	2,524	85	19,227
2017	18,764	277	3,401	85	22,527
2018	17,707	250	3,371	70	21,398

[1] Closed-end fund data include preferred share classes.
[2] ETF data prior to 2001 were provided by Strategic Insight Simfund.
[3] Total investment company assets include mutual fund holdings of closed-end funds and ETFs.
Sources: Investment Company Institute and Strategic Insight Simfund

---

[58] https://etfdb.com/screener/#tab=technicals
[59] https://etfdb.com/screener/#tab=technicals

The increased availability of other investment products has led to changes in how investors are allocating their portfolios. The percentage of mutual fund companies retaining assets and attracting net new investments generally has been lower in recent years. In 2018, 26 percent of fund complexes saw inflows to their long-term mutual funds; 75 percent of ETF sponsors had positive net share issuance (Figure 2.11).

FIGURE 2.11
Positive Net New Cash Flow to Long-Term Mutual Funds and Positive Net Share Issuance of ETFs
Percentage of fund complexes

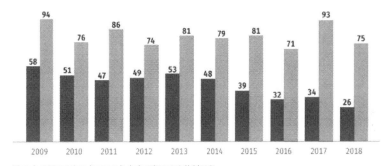

*Data for ETF net share issuance include reinvested dividends.

There were 9,904 ETFs worldwide by the end of August 2023. You name an investment category and there is an ETF for it. Wouldn't it be nice to know which ones of the 9,904 to invest in?

For simplicity in my analysis, I will use "ETF" to also include ETNs, so I do not have to say "ETFs and ETNs" every time I mention them.

Typically, when you buy an ETF, you get to invest in either the bullish side of the underlying asset or the bearish side, like the inverse mutual funds we just discussed. For either investment, you want the value of the ETF to move higher. This might be difficult to understand for some, so let me spend a little more time explaining shorting with ETFs.

Normally when you short a stock or commodity, you want the price of the asset to go down, so your investment goes up. It's the same with ETFs that short the market but with an ETF that shorts the market or a commodity or whatever the underlying asset is, as the underlying asset moves lower, your ETF price moves higher. Overall, ETFs provide an effective way to diversify and manage your own portfolio at a low cost.

For some, though, an index fund would be more apropos on the long side and an inverse fund on the short side, but having the ability to buy an inverse ETF when the market is tanking is a simple, inexpensive and potentially profitable way to hedge your long portfolio or just take advantage of a downward move in the market if not long anything.

Leveraged ETFs and ETNs

Because of the way these trading vehicles are created, leveraged ETFs do not represent the opposite of each other. This is important to understand. In fact, over time, both ETFs can lose you money. For example, let's look at the Direxion Daily Junior Gold Miners Index Bull 3x Shares (JNUG) and the Direxion Daily Junior Gold Miners Index Bear 3X Shares (JDST) seen in the graphic below.[60] One shows a loss of 79.73% (bull case) and the opposite of this ETF you would think should be up by that percentage amount, but was actually down 79.07%. How can this be if they are opposites? This is why for leveraged ETFs and because of the deterioration over time I only recommend you day or swing trade these for a brief period. Technically I do not recommend trading them unless you are an advanced trader.

Compare the performance of ETFs

JNUG	VS	JDST
Direxion Daily Junior Gold Miners Index Bull 3X Shares		Direxion Daily Junior Gold Miners Index Bear 3X Shares

Performance (100, 200, 260 Days)

JNUG Performance	JDST Performance
100 Days(-62.24%)	100 Days (-7.73%)
200 Days (-80.25%)	200 Days (-9.23%)
260 Days (-79.73%)	260 Days (-79.07%)

---

[60] http://www.nasdaq.com/etfs/etf-comparison.aspx

If you do choose to trade leveraged ETFs, then here are the 12 keys to success in trading leveraged ETFs.

1. Start with smaller shares if new to trading leveraged ETFs. Build to more shares and more risk as your account builds. Then diversify your trades. If you are trading leveraged ETFs, I recommend an account of 30k at least because of margin rules for accounts under 25k and your ability to trade in and out freely on a day-to-day basis. Less than 25k it becomes more difficult to trade and interferes with your decision making.

2. Be patient with the right setup. When sentiment is low, it may be the best opportunity to profit from a reversal, but until that time, the trend is your friend and if sentiment is moving higher, keep the trade longer but add a trailing stop.

3. Keep a stop when wrong (know your trading plan before buying a leveraged ETF). Some leveraged ETFs swing wilder than others, so their stops need to be widened. I have found that typically if you break lower by -2% to -3% the wrong way in a leveraged ETF you are in, it keeps going lower and lower. Same for breaking higher 2% to 3%. If you see what you are day trading break to a lower low for the day or the prior days low, why are you still long? Sell!

4. Add to a winning position (trend is your friend). If you are up 3% to 5% you can add to a position with a tighter trailing stop on new shares and move your original trailing stop on the first shares bought to break even. Look at the charts and the overall trend for confirmation and add shares if breaking the intraday high or prior days high.

5. Move stops up as your profit increases. Sell some shares on big spikes (see #6).

6. Sell 1/2 shares when profit goals are met. This can be as little as 2% when first starting out. There will be some runners at times, and you will find out that most of the time you do not sell, and get greedy, you give back the profit. Take profit. Make it a habit.

7. Once you sell 1/2 shares move stops up to break even on original shares. This becomes a no-lose trade once you do that. The more you are in no-lose lose trades, the sooner you will see your account take off higher. That is the goal.

8. Do not follow someone else's call blindly. Look at the darn chart yourself. Read a little about trading and moving averages and other data found later in this book and know that a little homework can go a long way for you.

9. Try a few of the trading services and see what suits you best and who is accurate. I purposefully do not have a chat room as it becomes addictive for traders (see #11). I know because I have been in them since 1999. I try to stay away from them and look at my own analysis first. The more I do that, the more I profit and the more I can go out and enjoy life. That should be the goal for everyone no matter what you trade.

10. Leveraged ETFs need to be monitored. If you must step away, use a limit order on your position. But it's best to sell your position if you cannot follow them closely and must go away for some reason (work or pleasure). If you want to swing trade something, go for the non-leveraged ETFs then you can go about your business that is taking you away from trading. I have set up the trading service for non-leveraged calls simply because most investors do not have the time to monitor the quick moves that occur in leveraged ETFs. You must be hands on when trading leveraged ETFs. Trading non-leveraged ETFs can be profitable as well.

11. Take breaks for exercise and family. Trading can be addictive. Eat.

12. Do not give up. Always try to improve and learn from your mistakes. Keep a journal of your trades. I have made every mistake I can make in trading. The hardest thing to do for you will be to keep a stop. If you do not, it is your one-way ticket out and back to your previous life. That is why it is good to do simulated trading, especially with leveraged ETFs. If starting with a smaller than 25k account, you must be more selective

on your entries into an ETF. Follow the trend trades first, then recognize that when everyone hates something, that is the time to consider it a buy, but only buy on days when the ETF is trading in your trades direction. Don't trade on margin until you are a seasoned trader.

You will find stories out there that talk about the underperformance of ETFs, but this is primarily related to those who buy and hold the leveraged ETFs, Again, I do not recommend holding leveraged ETFs for the long term because of the deterioration discussed earlier.

You will hear plenty of horror stories too about leveraged ETFs and you will not find any financial advisor recommend your average investor buy or trade them.

Occasionally you will see an ETN, not an ETF, blow up and XIV was one of those that I witnessed blow up live. But you would not have been long it to begin with based on the Trading Strategies and I would not fear such destruction with any of the high-volume ETFs.

Read the story at the footnote at the end of this sentence on what happened to XIV and you will get a feel for the extra risk you take on when you trade volatility.[61]

It is important you read the prospectus of anything you invest in, but again, with Trading Rules and the Trading Strategies, one cannot get stuck in a situation like what happened with XIV.

We are human and sometimes we make mistakes. When I stray from the rules, I typically do not make a profit. Stick to the rules and you will do fine.

For more on ETFs, I suggest you go to the NASDAQ site, and read the list of FAQs.[62]

---

[61] https://towardsdatascience.com/the-xiv-meltdown-1b0608110b9f
[62] http://www.nasdaq.com/etfs/etf-faqs.aspx#/

CHAPTER 9 - ALTERNATIVE INVESTMENTS

Emerging Markets, International Stocks, and International Bond Investments

Whether it is through mutual funds, bond funds or ETFs, you can invest in almost any country you wish. Emerging markets at times offer fantastic opportunities to profit, on both sides of the trade. You can go long on Vietnam, or short Russia depending on the geopolitical situations that arise. If a crisis develops somewhere then jump on that trend with an inverse ETF.

When markets trend, you simply trade with that trend and take profit from it. While this is what we discussed with U.S. investments, it can be said for international investments as well, especially when the U.S. stock market is falling.

If the trend begins to reverse you can sell or just use money management techniques like selling half after a nice run higher and letting the rest ride with the trend, selling shares incrementally and locking in more profit as the price increases. Or you can just use a trailing stop and go about your day. Your goal would be to sell the last shares just as the trend is peaking, but do not expect perfection. Coming close to the top is good enough. Then you simply look for the next trend. There is always a trend happening somewhere.

This is the beauty of active trading and taking control of your wealth. Whether it is U.S. markets or foreign markets, an investor should be trading without fear. We will talk more soon about the ins and outs of knowing whether a trend has started and when to get in and out. This basic knowledge is what can make trading fun!

Foreign Currencies

Most people in the U.S. keep their money at a U.S. bank, where it is subject to the risk of dollar depreciation. But there is a U.S. bank that is FDIC insured and allows you to invest in foreign currencies.

When I wrote about this in 2016, I recommended a company called Everbank which allowed you to hold your cash in one of many currencies, such as the Canadian dollar, Chinese yuan, or the Swiss franc, among others. Everbank was bought out by the large insurance company TIAA and that shows you the value they saw in what Everbank offered its clients. You can now buy foreign currencies through a CD that is FDIC insured through TIAA bank.[63]

There is volatility in these currencies, but there is also opportunity. From 2011 to 2014, the Chinese yuan moved higher against the dollar, but since has fallen with the tariff wars, as seen in the next chart.

CNY to USD Chart

4 Aug 2009 00:00 UTC - 1 Aug 2019 12:40 UTC **CNY/USD** close:**0.14487** low:**0.14339** high:**0.16555**

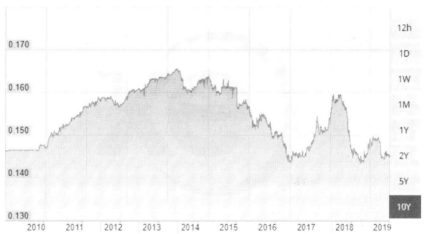

TIAA Bank foreign currencies will be subject to conversion rates that average 1% and while CDs have no fees, their Access account may be subject to monthly fees.

Why is this important to investors? If you have funds in a country's currency and that country has trouble on the horizon, you can easily switch your liquid cash over to a country's currency that is moving up in value. Many in foreign countries choose the U.S. dollar as a safe haven. But at some point, even the U.S. dollar could be in trouble with the mounting debt and being the world's largest debtor

---

[63] https://www.tiaabank.com/investing/foreign-currencies

nation. TIAA bank offers a way to move to other currencies that can move up when the dollar is falling. You can even diversify among a basket of currencies to improve performance.

Those in Argentina if they were able to do so, diversified out of their currency the peso as it went from $50 pesos to the dollar to its current exchange rate of over $900 to the dollar. Argentina however is implementing cuts to big government and might be reversing at some point.

Is your country's currency safe? Does it make sense to diversify if your countries Debt to GDP ratio is over 100%? Most likely it does. The chapter on gold and silver will shed more light on this.

You do not hear about investing in currencies because your broker does not make any profit from recommending it. They typically want you to stay in-house with their firm and invest in their money markets and the like. But even though these currencies may not be paying an investor much right now, there will be some leaders in the years ahead. Will it be those countries with less debt and more growth like the Chinese Yuan? Maybe. To have that account invested in Chinese yuan and have it FDIC insured could be a bonus to investors.

Real Estate Investment Trust (REIT)

When real estate is in a bull market, REITs are a wonderful way to invest and provide a good income return at the same time. What is nice about some of the REITs is that you can dive into the assets they hold, and make a judgment call as to whether those assets the REIT owns are poised to weather any downturn in the markets or a rise in rates. The REIT may have acquired the asset at a low price and the income may be enough to keep things afloat in the beginning as money is raised.

For example, let us say the REIT had as one of its assets a prison in Texas with 100% occupancy. You can speculate that the prison will be self-sufficient, and all bills paid no matter what the economy does. You can look at the long-term leases of buildings that the REITs own to see how many years of an income stream your REIT will provide. The longer the lease, the better the consistency of the REIT's return moving forward, especially if the tenants are businesses that have been around awhile.

A Word of Caution on REITs

Fed chair Bernanke's comments back in May 2013 led to a sharp selloff of Real Estate Investment Trusts (REITs) and some other asset classes, such as emerging market equities that were reliant on "easy money" from the Fed.

The Dow Jones U.S. Select REIT Index dropped 15.8% from its peak on May 21, 2013 (the day preceding the Fed comments), to its 2013 low on June 22. However, as markets calmed, the index recovered most of its losses by mid-July and reached new highs in 2014.[64]

Real Estate Investment Trusts are great investments in good times, but when Covid hit, it killed the REIT market. While no one really expected such a calamity, those who had REITs maturing were getting much less than what they invested. Being that one cannot exit a REIT till maturity, there are still many today who would love to have liquidity, but REIT's have zero liquidity. To make matters worse, many have lost the income from tenants going out of business or exiting to another state.[65]

The REITs have not recovered by mid-2024 with some decent dividends for some. There will be many investment advisors trying to sell these as they provide a great commission to the advisor, but there is some caution warranted to be sure.

Some history on REITs is appropriate here. REITs are typically illiquid, and you can lose principal. In 2013, the last episode of rising interest rates before the present one in 2023/2024, REITs, along with corporate and junk bonds, got hammered. The interest they generate can make up for some of the losses, but there is a good chance you will lose principal as rates rise.

Whether interest rates are rising or falling does not seem to be the key driver of REIT performance over medium- and long-term periods. Rather, the more important dynamics to address are the underlying factors that drive rates higher. If interest rates are rising due to strength in the underlying economy and inflationary activity, stronger REIT fundamentals may very well outweigh any negative impact caused by rising rates.

---

[64] http://us.spindices.com/documents/research/the-impact-of-rising-interest-rates-on-reits.pdf?force_download=true

[65] https://www.sciencedirect.com/science/article/abs/pii/S1544612321002129

You can see from the following chart, the fiscal crisis of 2007-2009 was not kind to REITs. We are close to that double top now, the same topping area you saw in many other charts in this book that would lead one to believe a recession looms.

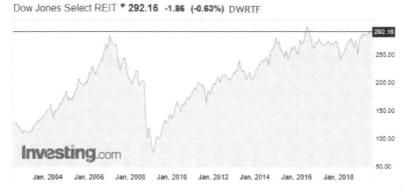

Dow Jones Select REIT * 292.16 -1.86 (-0.63%) DWRTF

The above chart was from November of 2023 and May of 2024 has fallen to 254.08 and presently trading at 273.74.

There are some of these REITs and Income Strategy ETNs that are currently yielding 8%-10% or more, but again, you must know your risk. Check out the following links to analyze what UBS has to offer that might fit your income needs or talk with your broker about the pros and cons of a REIT investment. It just may be that a future rate increase that can hurt bonds may not hurt REITs if you choose wisely.

http://etracs.ubs.com/product/list/index/assetClass/reits

http://etracs.ubs.com/product/list/index/strategy/income

http://etracs.ubs.com/product/list/index/assetClass/mlps

Treasury Inflation-Protected Securities (TIPS) and I Bonds

When you have an interest rate environment where there will be a mad rush to exit bond funds, there is still a need for a conservative investment that pays interest. You may need to purchase Treasury Inflation-Protected Securities (TIPS), or I Bonds to keep pace with interest rate increases, but they have shown to be a bit lagging.

TIPS

TIPS are expected to counter the inflation risk of your return and are guaranteed by the U.S. government. They are both liquid and exempt from state and local income taxes, but federal income taxes are paid the same year interest is received.[66] But even TIPS got slammed with higher rates in 2013, as they lost 8.5% that year.[67] TIPS were paying only around 3% when inflation was running around 8% in 2024.[68]

I Bonds

I Bonds are guaranteed to never lose value and track the CPI-U inflation rate. They must be held for a minimum of one year and are illiquid during that time. They are subject to a three-month interest penalty if redeemed within the first five years. The I Bond rate for Nov. 2015 – April 2016 was 1.64% and for May 1, 2019, through October 31, 2019, was 1.90%.[69] The rate has jumped to 4.28% in 2024 with the Fed raising rates.[70]

The major difference between TIPS and I Bonds is that inflation indexing is monthly for TIPS and semiannually for I Bonds. Also, TIPS are bought and sold in the secondary securities market, while I Bonds cannot be.[71]

Utilities and Energy-Related Investments

Energy is an area that I really like for the years ahead. Oil, solar, natural gas and utility companies are all good places in the longer term for assorted reasons. Oil, natural gas and utility companies can simply raise rates to keep pace with inflation. Solar has been good for years in saving homeowners and businesses the prohibitive cost of utilities, but government subsidies have helped this industry, and you will need to keep an eye on continued government investments here.

---

[66] http://www.investopedia.com/articles/bonds/07/tips.asp
[67] http://performance.morningstar.com/funds/etf/total-returns.action?t=TIP
[68] https://www.treasurydirect.gov/marketable-securities/tips/
[69] https://www.treasurydirect.gov/indiv/products/prod_ibonds_glance.htm.
[70] https://treasurydirect.gov/savings-bonds/i-bonds/i-bonds-interest-rates/
[71] http://www.ibonds.info/About-I-Bonds/Compare-I-Bonds.aspx

Nuclear energy-related companies are all a good place to park funds. Nations always will have a need for energy and some countries outside the United States use nuclear technology outside the United States as their main source of energy. The U.S. has ninety-three reactors in use followed by France with fifty-five and China with fifty-three. Russia had thirty-seven and energy starved Japan has thirty-three.[72]

I had a client who was in her eighties and many years ago who while a young college graduate, received a $50,000 gift from her father. She took his recommendation to invest in utility companies because they pay a dividend. That $50,000 gift she never touched and was proud of that. It had grown to over $3 million over her lifetime.

A couple of good utility plays would be Duke Energy (DUK) or the Vanguard Utilities ETF (VPU). Go to Morningstar.com and look for the utility sector mutual funds. Once there, click on each of the top five funds based on the last year and three-month returns, and look at their top holdings. It is one of the easiest ways to see which utilities are most popular to fund managers.[73]There is one energy investment that needs singling out, and that is oil.

Oil and other Commodities.

The price of oil falling to the lows hit in 2016 was a gift to investors. The following are ideal investments for oil ETF (USO), which tracks the oil price or any good oil company stocks in the United States like Exxon Mobil (XOM), which has good income and cash flow.

While most investors will buy large producers like Exxon, there are some smaller companies that might get you higher returns while shedding off some good income. A good site to find them is dividend.com and for oil companies, use this link: http://www.dividend.com/dividend-stocks/basic-materials/oil-and-gas-drilling-and-exploration/

OPEC is still the major player when it comes to price control. The following is an original sentence I wrote when I was doing the rough

---

[72] https://en.wikipedia.org/wiki/Nuclear_power_by_country
[73] http://news.morningstar.com/fund-category-returns/utilities/$FOCA$SU.aspx

draft of my book, "I imagine war will break out somewhere at some point and that in and of itself makes oil an attractive investment for years to come." We have since been involved in Ukraine and Israel conflicts and we trade it up and down and it typically has predictable patterns to profit from either way it goes.

Other commodities such as copper, steel, iron ore, aluminum, uranium, platinum, palladium, rhodium, and grains (we will deal with precious metals separately) are tradable using the trading strategies you will learn later in the book.

Infrastructure

Our cities are falling apart, so you will see more and more invested in infrastructure. Look for local companies, which always win the bids for city contracts. It will take some digging, but all of this is a matter of public record.

Go to your state's official website (your state, followed by ".gov") and search for "contracts" or "bid," and you will find a list of who is doing business with the state. You can also do a Google search for "bids and contracts" and the name of your city. Which companies are winning bids consistently because of their connections with the decision-makers? Some of these companies will be listed and you can buy them. Others will be private and not available to invest in.

For example, if you go to Michigan.gov and do a search for "contracts," you get the result "Contract Connect." When you click on that link, you come to a page where you can choose "Vendor Gateway." This page shows a link to www.Buy4Michigan.com. Click on "Active Contracts" and see who the city is doing business with. The first contract on the list is for Mental Health and Substance Abuse Insurance, with the vendor Magellan Behavioral Health Inc. A search for that company shows it is a listed company with the stock symbol MGLN. The contract date was February 1, 2014, and became a public record that day. The stock could have been bought the first day of trading after that approval by the state of Michigan for $59.55 a share. By April 1, 2015, the stock hit $71, a 19% return.

This is how doing a little homework can help your profit and shows how important it is to stay on top of the companies you are invested in by analyzing their quarterly reports.

Robotics

Many of you who are avid watchers of the TV game show *Jeopardy!* were impressed by the winning streak of contestant Ken Jennings—74 games in a row and over $3.1 million over a 182-day span.[74] Jennings and another contestant, Brad Rutter, who defeated Jennings in two *Jeopardy!* championship tournaments, were pitted against IBM's "Watson" computer, named after the company's first CEO, industrialist Thomas J. Watson. The computer was programmed to answer questions with only its four terabytes of disk storage and no connection to the Internet. Watson handily defeated the two former champions, for a $1 million prize.

This is indeed the rise of the machines I spoke about earlier and an age where computers are increasingly taking over the jobs of working Americans. Of course, another Jeopardy! contestant, James Holzhauer, was good at answering questions like Jennings but used a different betting strategy to make more money in a shorter time than Jennings. I like this guy as I find it a challenge to conquer things like trading with the right strategy.

Computers like Watson have evolved to taking on bigger tasks like utilization management decisions in lung cancer treatment at Memorial Sloan Kettering Cancer Center, in conjunction with health insurance company WellPoint.[75] Robotics technology is the wave of the future and necessary for your portfolio.

The market for robot systems is growing at a good clip and is expected to continue to grow, as shown in the following chart (naturally this is not a good sign for the manufacturing sector and furthermore contributes to deflation of jobs along with lower prices as a result).

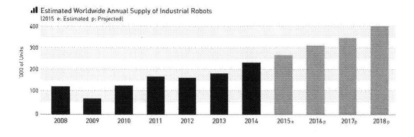

Estimated Worldwide Annual Supply of Industrial Robots
(2015 e: Estimated p: Projected)

---

[74] https://en.wikipedia.org/wiki/Ken_Jennings
[75] https://en.wikipedia.org/wiki/Watson_(computer)

Global industrial robot sales doubled over the last five years. Talk about a growth industry![76]

Asia is the strongest growth market (China, Japan, Korea) followed by the United States and Germany.[77]

There is a website that lists the top fifty robotics companies—some listed, some private. Understand this is a newer field and you will have to do research to learn more about it before investing. The *Robotics Business Review* provides you with RBR50 and considers these to be the most influential public and private companies in the global robotics industry.[78]

3D Printing

3D technology has revolutionized many industries, from car makers to aerospace and defense, as well as oil and gas. There is even the use of 3D technology for creating organs and tissues. 3D technology is here to stay and is a future growth industry.[79]

Some of the companies to keep an eye on are ExOne Company (XONE), 3D Systems Corp. (DDD), Stratasys Ltd. (SSYS) and Voxeljet AG (VJET).

One of the companies to watch regarding an IPO is Carbon3D https://www.carbon3d.com/ which boasts Google as one of its investors for its 3D printing technology. Their CLIP (Continuous Liquid Interface Production) technology is faster than standard 3D printing methods, printing in a fraction of the time.[80]

Trading Options, Puts, Calls, Futures

For serious traders, option strategies can offer hedging oppor-tunities against your present longer-term portfolio, say of index-related ETFs or funds but they are not for everyone.

---

[76] https://ifr.org/ifr-press-releases/news/global-industrial-robot-sales-doubled-over-the-past-five-years
[77] https://ifr.org/downloads/press2018/Executive_Summary_WR_2018_Industrial_Robots.pdf
[78] http://www.roboticsbusinessreview.com/rbr50
[79] http://finance.yahoo.com/news/3d-printing-stocks-near-52-200808555.html
[80] http://www.forbes.com/sites/aarontilley/2015/11/04/how-carbon3d-plans-to-transform-manufacturing/

John Carter, the author of Mastering the Trade is said to be one of the best option traders in the world. A trader I trade with was fortunate to have him as one of his mentors and was trading with him a few years ago when John made $1.4 million on a trade in TSLA in less than twenty-four hours. He had unfortunately jumped out too early but still did quite well in the trade.

He says that option trading is a fantastic opportunity to provide leverage to one's trading, as well as providing a myriad of hedging possibilities. There are over fifty individual strategies that can be deployed to achieve success while trading the various market conditions. There is something for everyone, depending upon their objective.

A couple of good books to read for reference that I have relied upon are The Options Playbook by Brian Overby Mastering the Trade (second edition) by John Carter, and Trading in the Zone by Mark Douglas that I recommend for some good guidance relating to trading attitude and discipline.

Options are bets on what an underlying asset is going to do in the future. Buying a call option at a higher price means you think the underlying asset is going to move up. Buying a put option at a lower price means you think the underlying asset is going to move down. The further out the option is from the current price, the cheaper it becomes. In volatile, quickly falling, or rising markets, you will find options can be more expensive because everyone sees the same potential move. It means you must pay more for an option out of the money as price is "expected" to move in that direction.

There is some validity to options, but for most investors, it is too complicated to explain without authoring a separate book. I prefer to leave this analysis for those who wish to do further research as experienced investors who have profited from the ideas from this book before diving into options.

Because trading options can be quite technical in nature, it makes sense to paper trade what you would do in advance of trading, keeping an eye on whether the bid and ask liquidity is there for you.

One can familiarize themselves with options as the next step in their education on the markets, but a trader can also look at unusual option activity to gauge potential price direction for their current trade potentials through the following footnote.[81]

Trading options and futures are VERY RISKY. I do not recommend it at all and the trading system I have researched does not recommend taking such a risk. Why take the risk that a futures contract can go negative like it did for oil? I am conservative when it comes to my trading service and the backtracking of the system is something that can be used in making future calls with minimal risk. But when you trade futures, you must understand stops are necessary when wrong. Emotions will come from everywhere keeping you in a losing trade and next thing you know you are blowing up your account. For this reason alone, I do not recommend futures but as you will soon see a diversified approach is better.[82]

For teachers to get their students involved in understanding investing at an early age, there is the Stock Market Game. This should be mandatory for all students, beginning at least in high school the first year which coincides with the legal age for getting a job and making money.[83]

Cryptocurrencies

The cryptocurrency craze is back in 2024 and is a viable yet unknown risk that underlies the industry. If you are going to trade cryptocurrencies, you can apply some of the rules outlined in this book for buying and selling. Most who dabble in crypto should only buy the most liquid, and the following top ten are good ones to trade if you choose to. Prices of course will be different depending on when you read this book, but these ten cryptos have been consistently in the top ten based on market cap.

---

[81] https://www.barchart.com/options/unusual-activity/indices
[82] https://www.marketwatch.com/story/oil-prices-went-negative-a-year-ago-heres-what-traders-have-learned-since-11618863839
[83] http://www.smgww.org/

#	COIN	PRICE	1H	MARKET CAP ▼
1	BTC	$66,895.00	▼ 0.2%	$1,319,397,274,857
2	ETH	$3,115.25	▼ 0.2%	$374,595,288,960
3	USDT	$1.00	▼ 0.0%	$111,387,086,868
4	BNB	$577.75	▼ 0.3%	$88,921,559,144
5	SOL	$171.27	▼ 0.7%	$77,041,855,340
6	USDC	$0.999474	▼ 0.1%	$33,454,231,226
7	STETH	$3,113.88	▼ 0.1%	$29,148,390,184
8	XRP	$0.521567	▼ 0.2%	$28,860,538,245
9	TON	$6.48	▲ 0.1%	$22,507,310,425
10	DOGE	$0.153050	▼ 0.1%	$22,074,687,931

Cryptocurrency is a digital payment system that does not rely on banks to verify transactions. It is a peer-to-peer system that can enable anyone anywhere to send and receive payments. Instead of being physical money carried around and exchanged in the real world, cryptocurrency payments exist purely as digital entries to an online database describing specific transactions. When you transfer cryptocurrency funds, the transactions are recorded in a public ledger. Cryptocurrency is stored in digital wallets. Cryptocurrencies run on a distributed ledger called blockchain, a record of all transactions updated and held by currency holders.[84]

Bitcoin is the most popular cryptocurrency and is even being adopted by some countries to replace their current currencies. But with that comes the risk of extreme volatility and thus Bitcoin does not make a stable currency, one of the requirements for a medium of exchange.

Being that cryptocurrencies are competition of sorts to central banks money monopolies, at some point central banks will have to do something to replace the local country currencies we know of today. In doing so, will choose from thousands upon thousands a new digital currency to present to the world.

As I wrote in my Illusions of Wealth book, every single currency throughout the history of humankind has failed without exception. Why? Because governments screw them up. This has happened in the United States before and our current currency experiment, the U.S. dollar, or Federal Reserve Note, which began in 1913, now has over $34 trillion of debt backing it. You can bet that cryptocurrencies are being looked at as an alternative currency.

If you are the central bankers of the world, or the elitists who run them, you are always looking for a plan B if the current plan A currency is not providing you with the same financially rewarding outcome as it has in the past. The Federal Reserve is already talking about central bank digital currency (CBDC) and claim that it would be "a liability of the Federal Reserve, not a commercial bank." They say that it will not replace cash but accomplish the following; "it could provide households and businesses a convenient, electronic form of central bank money, with the safety and liquidity that would entail; give entrepreneurs a platform on which to create new financial products and services; support faster and cheaper payments (including cross-border payments); and expand consumer access to

---

[84] https://www.kaspersky.com/resource-center/definitions/what-is-cryptocurrency

the financial system." They also say "a CBDC could pose certain risks and raise a variety of important policy questions, including how it might affect financial-sector market structure, the cost and availability of credit, the safety and stability of the financial system, and the efficacy of monetary policy."[85]

As an investor, you are not as concerned with which of the cryptos will be the chosen one, but how can you profit on trends. Sure, XRP many think will be the chosen one, or even Bitcoin, and you can park some fun money in them, but as a trader, you are looking for liquidity first and a trend to jump on. The underlying value of cryptos is different than stocks you buy of a company with assets. It is virtually supply and demand that drives price, and if you have a limited supply, then price can move higher and vice versa.

Unlike a tangible asset with limited supply, like gold or silver, which can be utilized for many things like medicine, machinery, batteries, etc., there is no utilization value for cryptocurrencies. There is blockchain technology that some cryptos possess which is an advanced database mechanism that allows transparent information sharing within a business network. The financial sector is relying on this technology increasingly and thus a blockchain technology crypto like Ethereum is the second largest in market cap.

To dive into the 1000's of cryptos that exist would take an entire separate book. But if you do want to trade cryptos I want you to think about only trading the most liquid and not take the risk of a smaller cryptos even though some may be valuable options to trade. Eventually I will run a trading service for them, like the stock trading service you will discover at the end of this book, using the same criteria I use for stocks. It will not be difficult to apply the rules to crypto and will help take the guesswork out of which cryptos to buy. Put some fun money into Bitcoin if it fell to under $5,000. Anything is possible with cryptos.

Where to Buy and Store Cryptocurrencies

Billionaire Mark Cuban lost $870,000 to a crypto fraud. If it can happen to him, it can happen to anyone. First off, I would not brag

---

[85] https://www.federalreserve.gov/cbdc-faqs.htm

that you own crypto currencies. Second, I would only store them in my possession, not at the place you purchased them.[86]

Coinbase is a listed company and I think a good place to buy and sell crypto. You would set up an account by signing up with your personal information. After funding the account, you buy the cryptos you want. Always use limit orders. These purchases can be kept online in a hot wallet, or you can transfer them to a cold wallet for personal storage. A cold storage product could be Trezor or Ledger Nano X among others that have its own private key that only you know and keeps it off the internet where others can hack it.

It is not as complicated as it might seem to set up a crypto account. Watch a few YouTube videos and read the free information at Coinbase and you will have an account set up in no time.

Lastly, I do like the idea of diversifying into several of the cryptos, spreading the risk. But also know that the government is watching and pull the plug on your online account so keep the coins in your wallet outside of the system. Also, work with a bank that allows crypto transactions.

Marijuana industry

There will be at times opportunities in the marijuana sector like there was in 2024. Out of all the different sectors to invest in, marijuana stocks were at their lows in early 2024 and then started to take off. There was plenty of opportunity once they took off. With the Federal adoption of laws that legalize marijuana on the table, this industry like all others will have standouts.[87]

Remember, this is going to occur as the government needs more things they can tax besides alcohol, cigarettes, and gasoline. You can find a list of cannabis stocks at the link. https://finance.yahoo.com/u/yahoo-finance/watchlists/420_stocks/

---

[86] https://economictimes.indiatimes.com/tech/technology/billionaire-investor-mark-cuban-loses-870k-in-crypto-scam/articleshow/103730136.cms?from=mdr

[87] https://www.yahoo.com/news/now-i-get-it-legalizing-marijuana-explained-when-126104093993.html

Chapter 10 - Gold and Silver Investments

Why Gold and Silver?

There are times to own gold, and there are times when it does not make sense to. Knowing where we are in the cycle dictates whether you should own gold or be in dollars or dollar backed assets. Many own gold as insurance no matter what the cycle. It gives them a little peace of mind owning real wealth just in case the US dollar started to have issues, which it has had several times throughout its history and presently has broken to a 3 month low in 2024.

Gold typically works inverse to the dollar. If the dollar goes down, gold goes up, as it did from 1971 to 1980 and 2000 to 2011. And when the dollar goes up, gold tends to go lower, as from 1980 to 1999 and 2011 to 2016. In 2017–2019 we saw gold rise a bit and the dollar fall just a hair.

Since 1971, the exception to this inverse relationship would be the 1985–1987-time frame, when the central banks of the world colluded to crash the dollar. This culminated in the 1987 stock market crash, and an era of dollar strength until the year 2000, when the dot.com bust happened and gold entered its bull phase through 2011.

Central Banks and Gold: Why Do They Hold It?

Virtually all central banks own gold, to give the illusion that it backs their various currencies. But there is no connection between gold held at central banks and the fiat money they print. In fact, there have been central bank agreements to sell gold for many of these central banks that finally ended in 2019. They recognized gold is heading higher.[88]

Gold's and Silver Price History

Year	Price of Gold (End of Year)	Price of Silver (End of Year)
2000	$274.45	$4.57
2001	276.50	4.52
2002	347.20	4.66
2003	416.25	5.96
2004	435.60	6.81
2005	513.00	8.83
2006	632.00	12.90
2007	833.75	14.76
2008	869.75	10.79
2009	1087.50	16.99
2010	1405.50	30.63

---

[88] http://www.gold.org/reserve-asset-management/central-bank-gold-agreements

2011	1531.00	28.18
2012	1657.50	29.95
2013	1204.50	19.50
2014	1206.00	15.97
2015	1060.00	13.82
2016	1151.40	16.37
2017	1261.05	16.16
2018	1247.92	14.69
2019	1523.00	16.37
2020	1895.10	26.40
2021	1828.60	23.35
2022	1824.32	23.96
2023	2062.92	23.79
2024 May 18	2414.33	31.45

Gold and the National Debt

Pricing currencies in each other is part of the greatest illusions of all time. It is the purchasing power of your wealth that matters, not valuing your weak currency versus other weak currencies. The world's currency ship is sinking, and the lifeboats are made of gold. It will take more of all currencies to buy gold in the future.

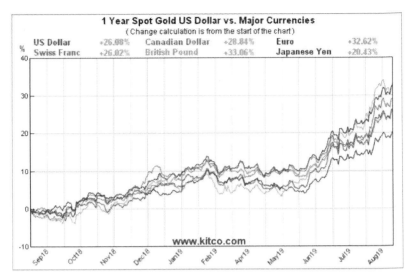

1 Year Spot Gold US Dollar vs. Major Currencies
(Change calculation is from the start of the chart)

US Dollar	+26.08%	Canadian Dollar	+28.84%	Euro	+32.62%
Swiss Franc	+26.02%	British Pound	+33.06%	Japanese Yen	+20.43%

www.kitco.com

1 Year Spot Gold US Dollar vs. Major Currencies
(Change calculation is from the start of the chart)

US Dollar	+26.08%	Australian Dollar	+36.77%	S. African Rand	+35.94%
Russian Ruble	+23.70%	Mexican Peso	+34.80%	Indian Rupee	+29.42%

www.kitco.com

In May of 2010 I had a table in my book Buy Gold and Silver Safely that you see below. It shows how much gold went up in the various global currencies. This was right before gold hit a high short of $2,000 an ounce. But ask yourself why gold would go up in price in all currencies? Do you see the illusion that currencies priced in each other really shows? And for most investors, they do not have precious metals as a hedge against this.

Gold's 10 Year Return through May 2010

U.S. Dollar	326.56%
Swiss Franc	176.31%
Canadian Dollar	194.61%
Euro	199.03%
Japanese Yen	267.39%
British Pound	322.72%
Russian Ruble	351.35%
Australian Dollar	173.53%
Mexican Peso	473.21%
S. African Rand	367.62%
Indian Rupee	337.84%

Gold has now taken off higher. It will not be a straight line up, but you can bet the national debt will continue higher. This is a good correlation over time signifying that gold will continue higher along with the national debt. The following chart covers gold and the national debt through 2023. Since the end of 2023, the national debt is up an additional $5 trillion and gold is up about $400. The correlation is spot on.

89 https://elements.visualcapitalist.com/visualizing-gold-price-and-u-s-debt-1970-2023/

What Is the Fair Value of Gold?

Because gold is a commodity, it does not pay interest. Some challenge the value of gold because it is difficult to determine, yet they ignore its history as money and ignore that it is difficult to determine the value of *any* commodity, yet the market does so every day.

The real issue here is not the commodity, but what the commodity is priced in: dollars, yen, euros, and so on. The commodity does not change. Gold will be priced higher or lower based on supply, demand, government policy, government debt, deflation, inflation, wars, interest rates, and so on. One way to value gold, then, is to price other assets in gold and see where they stand historically with their means. Why price in gold? Because it has been shown that gold is the more reliant asset to judge value rather than fiat currencies, all of which have eventually failed over time.

If you price other things in gold, you see where that asset is versus its historical norm because you are pricing it in your own country's currency. Let us look at what an asset priced in gold reveals to judge its value. We will do it with the DOW.[90] With this analysis, you are comparing one asset versus the other as to which would be better to buy.

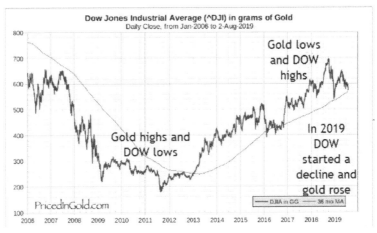

Dow Jones Industrial Average (^DJI) in grams of Gold
Daily Close, from Jan-2006 to 2-Aug-2019

---

[90] http://pricedingold.com/dow-jones-industrials/

DOW Priced in Gold (DJIA)

As you can see from the chart, the Dow is getting close to its resistance area priced in gold, leading us to speculate that gold may soon be the better-performing asset of the two and that is what we saw in 2019 start to occur. In fact, gold rose 18.83% in 2019 and 24.43% in 2020 and silver rose 15.36% in 2019 and 47.44% in 2020. The DOW fell during this time frame and since that time, even with the Dow breaking 40,000, priced in gold has not really moved at all in the last few years. If the gold price takes off higher here over $2,400, it is quite likely the DOW will fall from 40,000.

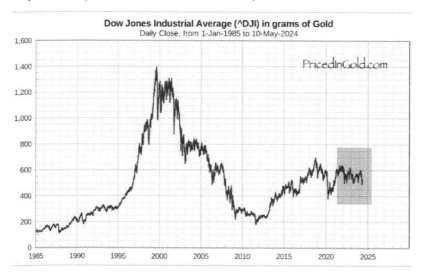

Gold and Silver Coins and Bars to Buy

The only type of gold and silver coins and bars to buy are the ones that with the lowest cost to the spot price of gold and silver. Forget collectible and numismatic coins and don't buy anything but bullion coins and bars.

For silver, it is the 1-ounce rounds and 1- and 10-ounce bars, and for IRA purchases, the 100-and 1,000-ounce bars. Silver American Eagles are the most popular, but not the lowest cost per ounce. Stay away from the 1.5-ounce Canadian coins that have a Polar Bear or some other animal on them. These are very highly commissioned silver coins pushed on the public by greedy gold dealers who claim they have value beyond the silver content.

For gold, the lowest cost metals are the 1-ounce bars and 10-ounce bars first and then higher premium Canadian Maple Leaf, and American Eagle coins (because these are the two most popular coins). But a kilo bar will be the cheapest if bought for one's IRA in larger quantities.

It makes sense to pay as little as possible for your gold and silver, but most investors just call a dealer up and buy whatever they recommend because they really do not know much about buying coins and bars.

What are the most popular coins in the United States? It would be the American Eagle Silver and Gold coins which are highly liquid, mostly because investors like the fact the US Mint creates them. Ironically, if you went to the US Mint online store to try and buy them, the premiums are typically much higher.

Gold in Your IRA/Roth IRA/401(k)/Transfer/Rollover

Many are not aware that they can buy physical gold and silver through a self-directed IRA or 401(k). This can be done through a transfer or rollover. The benefit of doing so allows an investor to have their metals appreciate tax free and eventually they can also withdraw the physical metals from their IRA and take possession of them if they choose, after the IRS gets their share.

Conclusion on Gold and Silver

It takes an entire book to cover the ins and outs of buying gold and silver and I address that in my book, *Buy Gold and Silver Safely which was updated in 2018*. This includes things like supply and demand analysis, storage issues, gold/silver ratio analysis, and questions to ask gold dealers so you know you will not get ripped off.

I will leave you with the one question to ask all gold dealers though:

If I buy this coin from you today at the current spot price and sell it back to you at the same spot price, what will you give me for it?

The gold dealer should quickly answer this question. If you see any hesitation or deference to anything other than a price or percentage answer, move on to a more reputable gold dealer. Remember, the dealer who advertises on TV and radio must pay a high price to do so. A reputable dealer cannot afford to pay for those commercials, so you must dig deep to find them.

CHAPTER 11 - REAL ESTATE

Real estate has always been a worthwhile investment for the long term, but like any investment, it has its cycles. Shows about flipping houses led to a new way of earning a living in America the last decade or so. We also have the US government thinking everyone should own a home and they have even set up assistance for lower income individuals to buy a house to fulfill "the American Dream." I do not view owning a house as being the "American Dream" it once was though.

Individuals have no business buying a house they cannot afford, government assistance or not. Other investors take on too much property as investments at the wrong part of the cycle and get killed. But both types of purchases of real estate can be great investments if your timing is right.

A house is an expense, a depreciating asset, and the bank takes years of interest paid by you—which ends up costing you much more than the original price of the home. The house and property must be maintained and insured, the sales commissions and fees to buy or sell in the future need to be paid and taxes take away from the profitability of owning a home. It all adds up.

To make matters worse, in the last year or so insurance premiums have skyrocketed and companies like State Farm and Allstate have been leaving certain elevated risk of calamity states like California. Nationwide and Progressive have announced changes to their presence in Florida. Insurance companies always have the flexibility to raise premiums or leave if they are not profitable. The homeowner pays the price.

Also, taxes go higher the more your home's value goes up. This drives some out of their home all together as their income is not enough to keep up with the taxes. This is inflation at its worst. It is also an overreaching government. Why do you pay taxes on a house you own outright? This tax is to cover public schooling, fire, police, and public safety departments. But the amount that is paid for some of these services is also out of control as are the pensions cities must pay out to government retirees each year. So do not expect any relief in taxes paid on your property.

Your hope is that you get out of the home you bought at some point with the appreciation in price you have obtained. Or, if you rent it out, more income than the expenses involved in maintaining the property is all you really need to supplement your retirement or lifestyle if younger.

A lot of that appreciation potential has to do with the timing of the purchase, which this chapter will address. I am not, however, addressing flippers in this section. Flippers are like those investors you see on TV shows who buy foreclosed homes at auctions, fix them up quickly, and dump them. They are a different breed of investor, and some do well, and some do not.

The Positives of Owning Real Estate

There are many reasons to own real estate, from the appreciation potential or the income it can provide if you rent it out or have rooms you can rent, there are also tax deductions for your mortgage against personal income although those deductions have been reduced and we will discuss that later.

You can even do well with real estate in this low-interest-rate environment if your mortgage payment is less than the rental income you receive. In this case, if you do not need to sell the property, you really don't have to worry about its value going lower. Your income versus expenses is what is important if you plan to keep the house for a while, giving appreciation a chance to catch up. But I would still prefer to buy low versus high in this case.

Here are some more positives for owning real estate:
- Can always rent out rooms to help with mortgage payment.
- Family members can move in if the economy gets worse, and they could help pay the mortgage down or provide extra income.

- Can have property with land to grow food (I do recommended investors own some land to grow food which is discussed later).
- Can make home self-sustainable with solar, reclaimed water, and other improvements to save money that you cannot do with a rental property.
- Do not have to worry about rent increases.

What Real Estate to Buy

Buying in areas with a history of maintaining growth or desirable retirement areas with moderate weather can keep prices buoyed despite an overall decline in real estate prices elsewhere. Buy apartment complexes that are not too old (higher maintenance expenses) instead of shopping centers, as shopping centers will be the first to go if/when the economy declines. Land and single-family homes are the worst investments to buy, as it is difficult to get any income from them. However the last few years companies like Blackrock have come in and bought many homes and apartment complexes, driving up real estate prices or raising rents above what their total costs to run the investment would be. Who is left holding the bag? The late to the table buyer of real estate. Don't let that be you.

You can always raise rents if the demand is there, which it should be, as more will be forced out of their homes again with the next economic downturn. Buy rental property in the right location near colleges, senior centers and where the cultural activity is prevalent.

We also need to address some of the problems with owning real estate.

The Problems with Owning Real Estate

Below is a list of what can go against your real estate investment:
- Property taxes can always go higher. Governments will always attach an overreaching arm to where the wealth is. They are even talking about raising capital gain taxes to 44%. While you get a $250k exemption per individual when selling or downsizing, anything above that would be taxed at this higher rate.

Hopefully, that never passes. Naturally, holding a living trust could exempt one from capital gain taxes upon the first passing if one wanted to sell then. Or upon the second to pass away there is another step-up pin basis.

- With the Tax Cuts and Jobs Act, one can only claim up to $10,000 in state and local tax deductions.
- Variable rate loan costs move higher with a rising interest rate environment. Those who took out adjustable-rate mortgages may not be able to afford higher payments, adding more inventories to the market and driving prices lower.
- The cost of insurance goes higher over time. Inflation is here to stay.
- Maintenance costs (heating, cooling, foundational, water damage and nature-related e.g., landscape maintenance and snow removal).
- Association dues and potential future assessments for condominium buyers. This area is getting out of control as inflation rises and the cost of everything goes higher. It can drive condominium owners or others that pay dues out of their home.
- Illiquid. If you need to raise capital and cannot qualify for a loan, and your home is the only place to obtain the capital, it may have to be sold at a discounted price to find a buyer who will take it on short notice.
- Even if you do not have to sell quickly, when the time comes, you still need a buyer at the price you want. The timing may or may not be in your favor, depending on the market in the future. If everyone is selling, you will not get the best price.
- Real estate commissions from buying and selling take away from overall profit but these commission are decreasing now to reasonable percentages. That is good news for the one selling and buying.

- When rates move higher, fewer will qualify to buy your home and as demand decreases, prices should fall.
- Poor job growth in the future and lower wages means fewer people will buy, and demand could fall.
- Real estate or land is never yours, as you can always lose it to the tax collector.
- Tighter mortgage rules can make it more difficult to enter the market, thus hurting demand.
- Buying condominiums in new complexes at the top of the market can leave you holding the bag for upkeep on other units should not all condominiums from the project get sold.

Benefits of Renting

No headaches of ownership listed above. If the rent is increased to where you cannot afford it, you can always move somewhere more affordable. You can even move to another country to save money—and use some of the savings to fly your loved ones in for a visit, especially if you move to a warm climate and your relatives have cold winters and want to escape. You may just find your quality of life improving a bit. This is discussed more later in the book in the retirement section.

Housing Bubbles

When the Fed lowers interest rates, their intent is to get the markets moving with a trickle-down effect. A housing market that is appreciating creates the demand for more housing-related goods, and subsequently Home Depot, Lowe's, and other companies are benefiting, more employees are hired, and the local economy improves with more spending by consumers.

However, if you interfere with the free-market rate to manipulate the real estate market demand with artificially lowered rates, there is typically a whipsaw effect, and that is what we saw with the 2006 housing bubble. We saw the Fed keep rates low, stimulating the housing bubble in 2006 and then their increasing rates that killed the housing market but there was also the double whammy of subprime lending and derivatives repackaging of these loans, which enhanced the crisis.

We had a nice bounce in real estate since the 2006 crisis, but it was fueled by quantitative easing and artificially lowered rates by the Fed, as they wanted to keep rates low to stimulate the economy. The fact of the matter, though, is that the economy did not grow, and the Fed could not even get 2% inflation out of it. Money velocity was going nowhere even if government printing of money was.

(skyrocketing M1)

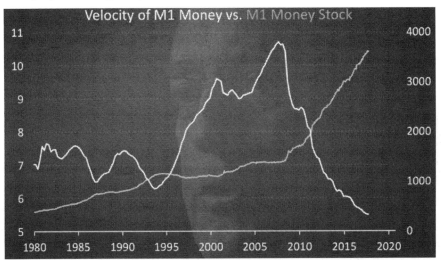

And even with this knowledge, the Fed raised rates in 2019 because they thought the economy was doing well, but the announcement killed housing and especially housing stocks. They then stopped raising rates, but the damage was done. Since then, the Fed is back at it with raising rates through July of 2024 and about at the end of killing the economy again. However, the damage is done and for the next few years the writing of a recessionary period is already appearing on the wall.

The American Dream?

Many may not feel like the home they bought is the American Dream as our government makes it out to be with all their programs to help people buy a home. Since the fiscal crisis, the home ownership rate has not even come close to where we once were. [91] We are still hovering around where we were in 2019 through 2023. Where is the demand going to come from to buy your house when consumers are at record levels of credit card debt and increasingly are losing jobs every week?

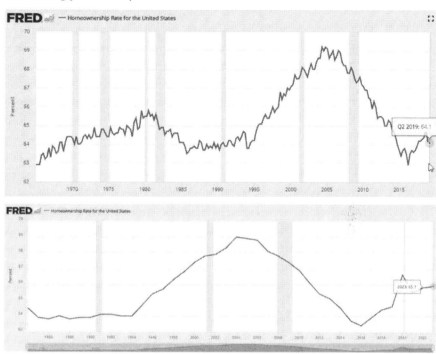

So that raises the question: When should you buy real estate?

When to Buy Real Estate?

The simple answer is to buy real estate when the market is dead, and no one wants to buy.

If you see the demand for electrical hookups increasing, that is a sign real estate is turning the corner higher. It is difficult to trust the data that comes from the real estate companies, so it pays to do your own digging and ask those in the trenches. You will also never hear a realtor tell you, "This is not a good time to buy."

---

[91] https://research.stlouisfed.org/fred2/series/USHOWN

When to buy:

1. Buy during the recovery phase: this is when you do not see cranes around high rises or new construction going on.
2. Buy where there is a restricted supply: California only has so much space, but many people want to live there because of the weather. Age sixty-five plus communities need housing care facilities, including hospice care. Buy close to these.
3. Buy where there is plenty of water or access to water.
4. If buying an investment property, be sure it gives you a decent 6–10% cash return above your costs.
5. Ask a realtor friend how business is (I say "friend," because it is more likely they will be honest with you).
6. Check the foreclosure listings for a trend. If the number is rising, the market is weak.[92]
7. One other consideration is will you ever be able to afford a home when rates move higher again. While there will be downward pressure on prices at first as the demand for homes will decrease because fewer can afford to pay the higher costs when rates rise, we will also have issues with falling wages and higher unemployment. But those who do manage to pay larger down payments or somehow pay cash for their home might be able to bottom scrape some good buys, especially at auction.

When to Sell Real Estate?

When the market is booming and everyone wants to buy. When there is oversupply and a strong amount of construction going on, sell. Also sell, when you begin to see median prices of homes fall after a big run up like we had in 2007.

---

[92] http://www.realtytrac.com/news/foreclosure-trends/midyear-2015-foreclosure-market-report/

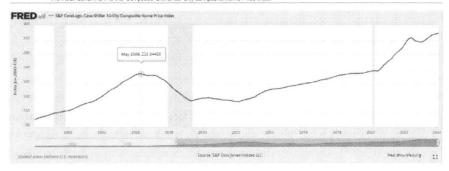

2015 YTD	2014	2013	2012	2011	2010	2009	2008	2007	2006	2005
Sept.	INDEX LEVELS									
5.83%	4.35%	13.38%	6.94%	-4.07%	-2.40%	-3.08%	-18.61%	-9.03%	0.67%	15.52%
Threat of higher rates	BENCHMARK* INDEX LEVELS									
5.47%	4.17%	13.54%	6.03%	-4.14%	-1.34%	-2.42%	-19.23%	-9.77%	0.22%	15.93%

* The index benchmark is the S&P/Case-Shiller 10-City Composite Home Price Index

You can see by the comparison of the previous charts that real estate prices are a bit out of control at present with the index at 337.84, compared to the peak of 226.64 before the 2006 housing crisis. The bigger the move, the harder the fall typically, but inflation is also part of the move higher. Things just cost more. The lumber, steel, and copper wiring cost more. The fixtures in the kitchen and bathroom cost more. Inflation can drive the price up but if everyone wants out at the same time, because the economy is crashing and the stock market nest egg or 401k you have is dwindling, the equity in your home is a place an investor will look to go. Timing the selling of your house and having a plan to cut down on your living expenses is something you need to prepare for now.

Of course, you can also judge the real economy for what it is and make that decision before the decline becomes apparent. Consumer debt levels were at record highs in 2019 and in 2024 even higher. Watch mortgage application trends for drops. Watch for higher interest rates which will put a damper on lending once the next Fed meeting occurs which will push rates lower for a short period of time.[93]

Do not listen to the experts (do your own analysis). Fed chair Alan Greenspan said this in 2005:

> *Although we certainly cannot rule out home price declines, especially in some local markets, these declines, were they to*

---

[93] http://www.cnbc.com/2015/11/25/mortgage-applications.html

occur, would not have substantial macroeconomic implications. In conclusion..., despite some of the risks that I have high-lighted, the U.S. economy is on a reasonably firm footing.[94]

I want to point out one other issue that you or someone you may know might come across in a downturn in real estate. If you can pay the mortgage, taxes, and insurance, you do not need to leave your home. During the 2006 meltdown in real estate, people were contemplating selling their homes because they were so far underwater. That is all fine to do if you can walk away from the debt and not worry about your credit score getting dinged and get into property again at some point at a lower price. However, people must consider getting out of a house that is heavily underwater versus the cost of renting for yourself or your family. It may make more sense to stay in the underwater house if your costs are going to be more to rent. That is a real-life dilemma for a few and in this case, who cares what the value of the home is? It is your overall expenses that matter.

That is why today, with such low interest rate mortgages, what you pay is more important than the value of your home if for some reason we have an extended downturn in prices. What is the rental cost alternative versus your low-cost mortgage that is locked in hopefully at a fixed rate for decades to come? How great is it that you can do better than the rental market where in the future there will be more rent increases?

When I first started my career in the 1980s, I remember some very smart engineers bragging about their 5% thirty-year mortgages. Lock in that low fixed long-term rate if the bank is dumb enough to give it to you.

Farmland: Always a Need for Food and a Good Source of Income

There is only so much land available to grow food and raise livestock. Every acre of land can earn your income, whether you rent it out for money or do the farming yourself. And for those of you who

---

[94] http://www.federalreserve.gov/boarddocs/Testimony/2005/
200506092/default.htm

believe Armageddon is coming, and I know you are out there, you can always use the land to live off. I know my mother told me long ago that she and my father would never sell the farmland we own, just in case we need to live off it someday. I do remember my mother's garden and how much food it provided, and you have never tasted such good, sweet corn as my father would bring from the field for dinner. I still like eating raw green beans to this day, because it reminds me of the "good old days" on the farm.

But now decades have passed, and my parents are getting to the 90-year-old range. They taught me the meaning of cash rent for your farm, and while they have seen the value of their acreage increase over the years, they have also seen their income increase. Farmland is an effective way to invest, as it gives you the potential of appreciation but also an income that can keep pace with inflation and the rising price of food. Whether you would need to go live on the farm and grow your own food and raise livestock is unknown, but it is hard not to like this type of investment.

Even beyond that, some of that farmland is being used to grow hemp which was removed as an illegal substance under the Agricultural Improvement Act of 2018, which federally legalized hemp and hemp-derived products that contain no more than 0.3% THC.[95]

Hemp can be refined into a variety of commercial items, including paper, textiles, clothing, biodegradable plastics, paint, insulation, biofuel, food, and animal feed.[96]

The Advantage of Owning Your Real Estate with a Living Trust

Most of you reading this have not taken advantage of setting up a living trust, but the reasons to do so are big time investment related, even if it involves the passing of a loved one at some point. So, this is especially true for those investors who are older.

The stepped-up basis I mentioned briefly earlier that you receive upon the first partner dying, can eliminate the capital gains tax if you were to sell your real estate (and stocks mind you) if it is owned by

---

[95] https://medium.com/cbd-origin/hemp-vs-marijuana-the-difference-explained-a837c51aa8f7

[96] https://en.wikipedia.org/wiki/Hemp

your living trust. This is the perfect time to consider a gifting program for children as well if the estate is large but consult with your tax advisor on what that can do for you. You would be handing over to your children the stepped-up basis of the property you are gifting. If they sold right away, there would be no capital gain tax, but it helps you reduce the size of your estate should it be large enough to generate an estate tax.

If parents outright gifted highly appreciated real estate (or stocks) to children, there could be taxes on any capital gain on that gift if sold because the child takes over the parents' cost basis.

There is nothing but advantages there for investors with such a small cost to set the trust up, but most do not take advantage of such planning. Make sure you get that done because there really is not anyone else telling you to do it or why.

Reverse Mortgage

Reverse mortgages may make sense for some individuals but one must beware of the pitfalls and get the family involved as they may lose out on inheritance. What is most important for the one with real estate is the ability to have a nice quality of life and that matters more than any inheritance potential.

A reverse mortgage is for those homeowners who have no loans on the property or exceedingly small loans to receive an income for life if they stay in the home or until they can no longer meet the obligations of the mortgage. This type of program is primarily for those who cannot afford to pay bills because of rising costs (inflation) from their current income and may want to get a boost in income without doing anything but tapping some of the home equity they have accumulated over the years.

The amount of income will be based on the person or person's age, current interest rate and value of the property. There is a maximum that can be paid so there may be better options if your home is worth more than $1,149,825 which I will mention in a moment. This figure increases every year. Weigh out these options.

One must read over the questions answered on the US Department of Housing and Urban Development website as well as a requirement for counseling from a HUD-approved agency <u>before</u> proceeding with a reverse mortgage.[97] There are also different payment plans based on whether you go with an adjustable-rate mortgage or a fixed-rate mortgage. With a low-interest-rate environment your costs will go up with an adjustable-rate mortgage and these costs will eat away at what is paid to you at exactly the wrong time, when items become more expensive. Now is not the time to choose the variable option.

A better alternative to a reverse mortgage might be where one could receive a monthly annuity and be able to receive that income for the rest of their life and still stay in the home. This will be discussed next.

Planned Giving and Real Estate

There are good alternatives to reverse mortgages through some established charities that will provide many more tax advantages and income choices for you. You can contact your favorite charity directly or learn more about what options you have through an advisor who specializes in this area through the Planned Giving Design Center which has the world's largest community of planned giving professionals.[98]

I at one time was a Certified Specialist in Planned Giving (CSPG) and it would take an entire booklet to give you all the various options available for charitable planning, but there are trusts available for those in retirement who might need extra income and their wealth is tied up in their home.[99] I'm sure for some of you, older family members may be in this situation.

Briefly, with these types of trusts one can receive a life income and still live in their home till they pass away or must be moved to an assisted care facility. Again, quality of life is what is most important here, not the inheritance a family member may receive. Most want

---

[97]

http://portal.hud.gov/hudportal/HUD?src=/program_offices/housing/sfh/hecm/rmtopten

[98] http://www.pgdc.com/

[99] http://www.plannedgivingedu.com/subs/certified.shtml

to live in their home till the day they die, and this is a way to do it and tap the equity in your home to live off and improve quality of life.

The downside of course is upon passing, the charity receives the house, so there must be some charitable intent. And the charity you choose must be able to afford the lifetime payments, so you will need to do your due diligence on their financials. There are ways however to continue the stream of income for heirs.

You would be amazed at all the benefits a charitable trust provides even for you as an investor. There is a reason you see CNBC Jim Cramer's disclosure say, "Jim Cramer's charitable trust owns this." Again, too much to go into here but if you are also in need of tax deductions because of the sale of other property, for example other real estate you own or highly appreciated stocks, then this is one way to wash out the taxes, especially if the government decides to implement a 44% capital gains tax rate.

Chapter 12 - Life Insurance and Annuities

I happen to understand the life insurance business quite well, as I was a part of the industry for more than a decade and have tracked it since. The industry itself is all about commissions, as that is how their agents get paid. Insurance agents are entitled to make money as they do help with family planning, but what they sell you is important to understand.

I remember decades ago, most of us in the insurance industry were taught to sell cash-value life insurance. It did offer much better commissions over selling term insurance. But then an upstart company called A.L. Williams came along with a multi-level marketing approach with a mantra of "buy term and invest the difference." It cut to the heart of the insurance industry, as investors got out of their cash-value policies and bought the cheaper term products. But the A.L. Williams agent took the saved money and sold the individual the lousiest mutual funds on Earth at the maximum commission allowed (8%), and that business model was short-lived. A.L. Williams eventually became Primerica.

I personally believe in the "buy term and invest the difference" philosophy as I do not want an insurance company in control of my investment decisions with products like whole life or universal life. But there is one aspect to using a type of hybrid insurance product called variable life that allows you many different investment options within your policy that may make sense for some.

If you fund the variable life policy at the maximum allowed under Section 7702 of the Internal Revenue Code (IRC), you can turn your insurance policy eventually into something other than insurance. You put as much money as possible into the life insurance policy without it becoming a taxable event under the IRC. At some point in the future, you can withdraw the funds tax free by loan to pay for children's education, take a trip, buy a car, or put a down payment on a house or an investment property. In a sense, you become your own bank and do not have to sell investments and pay taxes on the capital gain to get at your money. The funds grow tax deferred, but you have access to the funds at any time tax free. There is a small loan fee, but the loan can be paid off at your leisure. There are of course the fees associated with life insurance, but this type of planning is under-appreciated. Most insurance representatives sell the products where you pay as little into it as possible for a cash value policy and that is what makes no sense. Just buy term insurance if that is the case. Insure for the number of years you need coverage, like until your kids graduate college. After that, a little bit of term insurance to pay off the mortgage on the home in case a spouse dies.

Eventually this same cash value policy you have built up over time can be used to supplement your retirement through a series of loans calculated to last your lifetime—and you never have to pay the loans back. The funds paid to you reduce the death benefit upon your passing. This type of planning allows you to choose your income from a tax-free source, the insurance contract, in high-tax years or from taxable accounts like IRAs in low-tax years. It is nice to have a choice!

The only caveat is you cannot let these policies lapse by taking out too big a loan before you die because taxes will have to be paid on any gain over your cost basis. These are insurance policies, so if you do pass away before mortality tables say you should, your heirs receive a death benefit free of income tax as well, but that is not something you plan to happen of course. This type of policy would be included in your estate for estate tax purposes.[100]

Not all policies are the same, so look at several policies and their fees before diving in. Insurance agents make a hefty commission on this for a reason, but this is calculated in the premium you pay. There are no-load insurance policies out there, so you will have to dig deep in research to find them. You can read more about this in the linked footnote.[101]

One thing insurance companies have on their side that most other businesses do not is that they can always raise rates, insurance

---

[100] https://www.law.cornell.edu/uscode/text/26/7702
[101] https://www.fa-mag.com/news/here-come-new-no-load-insurance-policies-39476.html

costs, or fees if things do not go their way. Try to stick with a company that has a history of sound financial progress and low fees. Charlotte, NC-based TIAA-CREF Life Insurance Co. is one of those companies offering no-load life insurance.

Annuities

The Rolling Stones went on tour in the summer of 2019 and had only one sponsor: the Alliance for Lifetime Income, a nonprofit organization formed by a group of financial services firms to raise awareness about protecting income in retirement. There may or may not be a place for annuities in your portfolio moving forward, so this section will help you decide.

Insurance agents are also known to push annuities on their clients. I say "push" because these products are sold to investors, not bought by investors. Most investors do not rush out and tell their financial advisor, "I want to buy an annuity." They are sold primarily by insurance agents but also financial advisors looking for a quick good commission.

Many who sell annuities will push the higher-commission products which have longer penalty fees associated with them making them less liquid. You may not see the commission come off your initial investment, but it is calculated into the product in a deceiving way. The insurance agent will say the annuities are "no load" but you can assume that whatever the first-year cost of cashing in the policy if you were to cash out the same day you bought it, your agent is making 50-100% of that difference of what you would receive and the amount you invested. Sometimes this commission amounts from 8% to 15%. The way to figure this out is to ask your agent, if I bought this annuity today and sold it tomorrow, how much would I get for it? Your agent will not want to answer that question.

Annuities, whether fixed or variable, are ways for you to have your after-tax money grow tax deferred in an account that pays you a flat rate (fixed) each year or a variable rate based on the investments you choose, like the variable life insurance policy described earlier. Unlike CDs at a bank, an annuity is taxed only at the time of withdrawals on a LIFO basis. All earnings are taxable, and your principal is returned to you tax free.

The fixed annuity may or may not have an inflation protection aspect, but if it is an option, take it.

Fixed annuities were an excellent product to own in years past because they had a high minimum guarantee of 3-4%, and those who bought those policies were incredibly happy with them in the latter 2010s as interest rates kept moving lower and lower as we progressed into the year 2020. Fixed annuities also were unaffected by the 2006 fiscal crisis and that was a benefit of ownership. However, when interest rates rise, those who have a fixed annuity will find that their rate of return may not keep up with simple investments in market CDs, and worse yet, they could have what is called a market value adjustment (MVA) that can hurt their return if ever cashed in.

With a MVA for an annuity, if you surrender your policy or take out more than 10%, there may be an adjustment—higher or lower, depending on what interest rates are doing. It works like owning a bond and selling it. Overall interest rates have fallen in the last ten years into 2022. If you bought an annuity in the last ten years, and have an MVA policy, you may want to convert it now to a non-MVA annuity via a 1035 tax-free exchange to not pay any income taxes on it. You will receive a bonus that you may not know is there waiting for you. Check with your policy contract and talk to your insurance representative.

But if you hold on to your MVA annuity and eventually surrender it or take out more than 10%, the annuity holder may owe the insurance company money, which will be subtracted from the surrender value. Many are not aware of this.

It is for this reason I am not a fan of any MVA annuities moving forward. Interest rates will be moving higher, and I am not even a fan of fixed annuities because I do not think they will keep pace with the pace of interest rates moving higher. Just like with TIPS described earlier, fixed annuities that have an inflation adjustment incorporated into them will not keep pace with the real inflation rate.

The tax deferral benefit for annuities is good, but you will eventually have to pay taxes yourself on withdrawals of that money as ordinary income taxes, at a higher tax rate than today if our government cannot get a handle on their finances, which is the case. Your heirs would also have to pay taxes on any of the accumulation of these policies as they do not qualify for a stepped-up basis like bonds or stocks would. That is not really a good thing either.

If I chose to get an annuity because of the benefits of having a family that lives longer than mortality tables say they should, I would choose a no-fee variable annuity where I can control investment choice, not the insurance company, and one with an inflation rider to keep pace with inflation once I decide to retire and start taking a steam of income.

Funny story. While rewriting this book at one point while in seclusion, I did not have a television to watch and on YouTube they have some old movies from the fifties, and I was watching one called Red Planet Mars made from the year 1952. It was about the gentlemen who made first contact with Mars, and in their conversations back and forth, it was said that those on Mars live to age three hundred on average. It was then a ticker tape had the following message come across the wire: "All life insurance companies today canceled the writing of annuities." I had to laugh at that one.

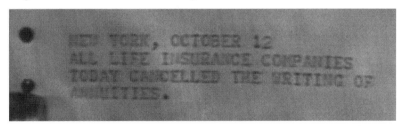

Just remember, insurance companies are always in control of your wealth, and I would not put all my eggs in an insurance company basket, even if you do have a family tree that lives longer than average. The contracts always state what changes an insurance company may make down the line. Read them carefully before committing your wealth to them. Remember, when things get tough for an insurance company, they abandon the policy holders.

Mutual Funds in an Annuity Wrapper

Variable annuities are mutual funds wrapped inside an annuity and are sold by insurance representatives and other licensed brokers.

They are either bought with after-tax dollars and grow tax deferred or can be purchased inside your IRA or 401(k). There are also hybrid index annuities that offer a percentage of the growth of a stock mutual fund investment (most common option) with guarantees built in to protect the investor from any market downturn.

These variable annuities add another layer of fees, called mortality and expense risk charges, in the range of 1.25% per year on your account value, or $125 per annum on a $10,000 investment. This fee takes care of insurance costs because the annuity is an insurance product.

Variable annuities may show an illustration that does not include the commission paid to a broker but includes it as a percentage of the amount invested, which can vary from 1% to 18%. These annuities may seem to be no load, but insurance representatives do not work for free. They get a portion of that fee, and it comes in the way of potential liquidation penalties, which are there to keep you invested with the insurance company.

The liquidation penalty, if you were to need to get at your money, can run quite high, typically 5–10%, if you need your money within the first five to ten years. The higher the liquidation fee on an annuity, the more the insurance agent makes. We briefly addressed this earlier. There are plenty of annuities out there with zero to exceptionally low liquidation fees, however. You do not hear of them because the insurance representative does not make money selling them. Again, annuities are sold not bought.

The penalty for withdrawing your money before age 59 1/2 is an additional 10% from the IRS should you need your funds. These are not liquid investments.

Annuities are tax deferred and unlike investing in mutual funds, your growth is not taxed as a capital gain when withdrawn but at the higher ordinary income rate. The gains, if any, on the annuity, are added to your current income for the year you withdraw which can push you into a higher tax bracket.

Variable annuities also make zero sense inside of your IRA or 401(k) because of the additional fees, but increasingly companies are going this route for their retirees. Save the fees and invest in low-fee products, unless you know you are going to live to the age of 90 or 100 and can take advantage of lifetime income options that beat the mortality tables actuaries draw up.

If your company only offers the annuity option for a 401k, do not roll it over into an annuity. Make sure you can get all your money out and roll it over into your own self-directed IRA where you can choose the investments. You do not want an insurance company in control of your financial future.

Immediate Annuities

You will see many commercials pop up on CNBC and other financial networks trying to get you to take out an annuity and receive a lifetime income from the money you deposit into it. This means they will typically pay you a fixed amount for the rest of your life: an income you cannot outlive. It sounds attractive, as it takes away the worry of how you will receive income in the future, but there are problems to be aware of.

Most immediate annuities will not keep pace with inflation. If the inflation rate goes higher and things cost more, your income will stay the same. You do not want this kind of investment today with such a historically low-interest-rate environment. Even those that have an inflation rider will not keep pace with real inflation, but it is better than nothing. The other problem is if you die, your heirs receive nothing, unless you choose to take a lower lifetime payout and provide an income for a spouse for their life or a specified period. In other words, you receive less to protect your spouse so they can continue to receive income for their life.

Another thing that makes it seem like immediate annuities are attractive is the income they pay you. It will be higher than any treasury or bond you can get in the open market on a fixed basis. Why is this? Because the immediate annuity pays you back some of your principal, too. This is what makes them look so attractive. It is the combination of a low interest rate plus your principal, calculated on how long the insurance company says you will live based on mortality tables that dictate how much you will receive.

One good thing about annuities is that if you are going to leave your children a lot of money and they are not good at handling it, leave them the stream of income only an annuity can provide upon your passing, but include the inflation rider. It is an income they cannot outlive, and it keeps them afloat. No matter how bad they are with finances, a check will always come every month. It is better than them squandering it, in which unfortunately many who inherit wealth will do.

You can look at the multi-million-dollar lottery winners and many professional athletes to understand how bad some are at managing large sums of money. I personally believe the first thing every professional athlete should do with some of their windfall is buy an annuity that will pay them an income for life. For $1 million put into an immediate annuity, a twenty-year old would receive a payment of $53,303 a year for fifty-seven years, their life expectancy. That is $3,038,271 over their lifetime. I bet many former athletes today wish they would have done that.[102]

Insurance Company Ratings

If you are going to be paying money into a life insurance policy for many years or taking out an annuity where you want the money to be there when you need it now or in the future, you want to make sure the company you are doing business with is financially sound.

There are several agencies that rate insurers in various categories. AM Best is the most popular rater of insurers, but you can also get ratings analysis from Fitch, Moody's, Standard & Poor's, and Weiss Ratings. Stick with the highest-rated companies with a sound balance sheet.[103] But take it one step further and see what their actual portfolio of investments consists of. Also, are they life insurance only insurers, or are they subject to high-cost property insurance claims by covering areas that are subject to natural disasters like hurricanes? If large enough, these natural disasters can do considerable damage to an insurance company's balance sheet.

---

[102] https://www.dinkytown.net/java/ImmediateAnnuity.html
[103] http://www.insurance.wa.gov/find-companies-and-agents/financial-rating-services/

Look at their bond portfolio average weighting. Those with shorter bond maturities should be able to keep pace with eventual higher interest rates. Those with longer-term maturities may be playing catch up and take more risk to maintain their profitability to keep paying their current policyholders. Of course they can always just pay the policyholder a lower payout. Insurers make all the rules and are in control of your future.

CHAPTER 13 - TRADING RULES

Rules for Trading ETFs and Stocks

Keep in mind that the trading rules for leveraged ETFs are separate but still use the same basic rules below:

1. Always have a plan for trading the day prior to making any trades. Most of the time your plan is based on sound tactics, but price movement can make any plan invalid if it wants to. Trust your plan, not what others say. Other voices will distract you. Trust your homework and trade your plan. Most importantly, don't be lazy when trading. Don't lie in bed and think you got this if day trading. You don't. It's akin to gambling and gamblers lose.

2. When opening a trade, make sure it is in line with the trend as this will increase your odds of success. Do not trade against the trend. Day traders may have short-term trades against the trend, but this is where you must distinguish what type of trader you are: swing trader or day trader for that trade. See #1, what is your plan? Do not fight the overall trend or the sector trend you are trading. Do not add to losing trades. Note: this is an important rule that must be adhered to in every trade. Trade with the trend! It is that simple!

3. For day traders and swing traders, trade with a goal in mind to lock in profit for half shares. Sell half the shares after a nice move up, especially a spike up, then move your stop to break even. You cannot lose on the trade if you do this.

4. Keep your pre-planned stop no matter what. Treat your stop as if someone is standing over you with a fly swatter and is going to keep smacking you every five seconds until you hit the sell button. Do not second-guess your plan. Emotions will play tricks with your mind to stay in the trade. The key to your staying in the game is to protect your account from

doing stupid things like not keeping a stop. It is the only reason you will fail at trading. And it happens more than one thinks. Do not be that person who does not keep a stop. I have gone as far as to debating hiring someone, telling them my plan for the trade, and then instructing them to strike me with that fly swatter every five seconds until I sell. That is how tough it is once you are in the trade to control your emotions and take a loss. The beauty of trading is there is always another day and another trade. Take the loss and smile as you know your success rate is dependent on this one rule. If you break this rule more than once, turn your account over to a trusted advisor. You are not cut out for trading.

The old saying applies here: "Markets can remain irrational longer than you can remain solvent." Know what your maximum loss for one trade is and do not break this rule. Never should it be more than 10%. Some say 8% and if conservative, 5% on a trade. If you are beginning trading, 5% is your stop out as your goal is to preserve your account when you start trading. This does not mean 5% of your account but 5% of the 1/10 or 1/20 or 1/100th of your account that you are trading on this one investment.

Once you are making good trades you can let your stops widen a bit if your trading plan is still intact as you are trading with house money. But do not get cocky and stick with the plan even if you have done well. Many days after a very successful day of trading, I gave back some profits because of a looser application of the trading rules. Really watch out for your own complacency once you have a good day of trading.

When utilizing a stop, if you put in a limit order for your stop out price, market makers can see it on the level 2 screen and come down and hit it and reverse the market right back up leaving you with the loss. The system you use for this stop out once your price to sell is close, must be a market order. The buy volume should be large enough to exit with a small spread if your stop out price is triggered. Do not just give market makers your shares by exposing your trade in advance with a limit order that everyone can see.

5. Have patience for the right trade. You will find yourself bored and want the trading action. This is gambling, not trading. Do not gamble! If not sure what the market will do in the short term, wait. Let the trade come to you. If unsure of direction, be patient for the setup that has all your indicators to buy aligned.

6. Never chase price higher unless you have a great reason for doing so. News events will get an initial spike and you chase it and then it reverses. Only things like a Fed policy change after an interest rate decision or something major would cause a trader to chase, especially if the asset moving higher has been beaten down. You can chase smaller shares and add if the trend takes force or if it dips and you have had time to analyze your indicators as to if a new trend is forming.

7. When in a trade as a day trader, make sure you are not distracted. If distracted, it is best not to trade. You can always come back to trading.

8. Never trade emotions. Fear and greed are your worst enemies when trading. Never trade when not feeling well or when angry, sad, upset or fighting with a spouse.

9. Targets that others give are irrelevant to your trading plan. Certain prognosticators who have a great track record will say such and such will go to a higher price and next thing you know we are breaking to a new low because of some news event. You would have been out if long and trading your plan and readjust. The higher price may still come, and you will have bought in at a lower price and made more profit trading your plan or have taken that capital while they are waiting on a higher price and profited from another trade. Sitting through downturns with your capital tied up is an opportunity cost lost. Trust your plan and implement it and move on to the next plan.

10. Losses are part of trading. Get used to them. But keep them small.

11. If you are uncertain about your trade and what is happening with the markets, and you are the slightest bit confused about your plan, do not hold it overnight or over the weekend. Getting out of the trade is ok. On to the next trade.

12. Watch for volatility during Fed interest rate decision days when Fed minutes are released. These are extremely volatile days. Even experienced traders wait for the trend to develop post-Fed meetings and minutes release dates.

13. Keep an eye on the economic data for the week and how it might affect the trades you are in.
    Economic data days like PPI, CPI, nonfarm payrolls, and unemployment data will whipsaw the market. You can see the calendar of upcoming economic data by going to this link at Investing.com, provided with the trading service. https://www.investing.com/economic-calendar/

14. Do an end-of-day review of your trades and compare them to your trading plan. Did your target buy and sells hit your price level? Did you execute or were you not paying attention and missed it and bought at the wrong price? Was this a short term (day trade) or longer term (swing trade)? If you made a bad investment, did you get out quickly or hold it as it went down?

15. Know when markets are most volatile. The first hour of trading is the most volatile and the half hour before lunch and half hour after lunch (12:00-1:00 Eastern time is market maker lunch). Also, the last half hour of trading can be volatile. Normally after the first hour the trend for the morning is set and you can ride what is up higher or down lower. The last hour of trading for each day is what you should try to stay away from. It is when many investors give back their profits for the day. Most profits for day traders are made in the morning. They trade and move on to enjoy the day doing something else. Countless times I have been up in the morning only to give it back. Don't do this.

16. Many investments you trade will gap up in the morning pre-market, open and then fill the gap back lower a bit before taking off higher. You typically can buy that dip if it fits into the overall trend where you were already in the trade from the prior day. Then you can debate on taking profit if it gaps up, depending on whether it is a day trade or longer-term swing trade.

17. Most of the money is made in trading in the morning session. You could just trade the morning market session and go golfing or hit the beach or go fishing the rest of the day. No rule says you must stay at your computer the entire trading day. Trade the morning session and go enjoy life. Do not give back profits you already made because you are bored. Do not let trading become an addiction. Live your life. Keep family first.

18. Trading pre-market and post-market can be extremely rewarding and very risky. Volume is lower and sometimes market makers push the market one way pre-market only to flip it after the market opens. The same rules above apply to trend, but your spreads on the investment may be wider pre and post market with the market illiquid to trade. Make sure you are trading something that has enough liquidity to exit the trade should you have to. News can cause you to keep a stop but the bid for your investment may be well below where the stock price closed and you become stuck till the next market opens for your exit. News is part of trading, and you cannot predict overnight news that goes with or against your trade. You can only trade what you know works and stick with your plan and adjust if something goes wrong with the plan.

19. Beware of what I call "professional's days." These are days when nothing is going the same way as it has been with your trading. What worked the day before does not work the next trading day. These are days when the market does the opposite of what is expected, and the "professionals" mix up the trading they have been doing to get traders to

sell their positions or cover if short. Best to find something else to do that day than watch the churning of one's account occur. This is where you learn not to overtrade for the sake of trading. What does your plan say to do? And this is where your patience comes into play, waiting for the right setup. Only day traders have to be concerned with this rule. The trading service is set up to not have to worry about this rule or rule #18.

20. You will find yourself listening to what others say and want to trade on their speculation rather than follow your own proven system. Or you will hear news that will shake you out of a position. Follow price action and the data and you will keep yourself from making mistakes.

21. Check your greed at the door. If you see a sell signal and are up nicely on the trade, holding out for a bit more can see a reversal come quickly. Stocks fall faster than they rise, so trying to get a few dollars more typically is not worth the effort. Move on to the next trade.

22. Holding trades for longer than 365 days means you get a lower capital gain tax versus holding them under 365 days. If you are close to capturing that tax advantage and get a sell signal, weigh the advantages of holding a few more days to get the lower tax rate on a sell. Short-term capital gains taxes range from 0% to 37% and long-term capital gains taxes run from 0% to 20% unless some administration changes this.

23. Remember, you can take profits on a trade at any point in time. There is no set formula for taking profit. But to cut losses you need to keep that stop at a certain amount or percentage depending on the size of your portfolio. No exceptions.

24. When you buy into a low volume stock or after-hours futures trading, the professionals know when retail is going long or shorting and will quickly try and whipsaw you out of a trade. Best to trade during market hours to avoid this whipsaw.

25. Most of you have not experienced a prolonged bear market and that's why I wrote this book.
26. When in a trade, look at those multiple timeframes to make sure your trade is with the trend. For day traders look at the 5 and 5 minute chart for trend.
27. If trading cryptocurrencies, expect wild swings at any point in time. Make sure you have liquidity in your trade by staying away from the smaller volume cryptos.
28. Cash is a position waiting for an opportunity. Be patient for an opportunity. A crash in the stock market is a gift to investors who have cash to deploy.
29. The 2-year 10-year inversion of yield curve then comes a recession. Keep an eye on it. If this goes higher than 0.0, watch out. We did come close with the early 2024 August downturn.

30. If trading with margin, know your risk. The easiest way to blow through an account is to jump right into trading with leverage in a margin account. You can lose money on an investment much faster than simply buying and holding a trade when you get signals.
31. Stay away from investments that are there to make the creators wealthy, not you. This includes NFT's or

Nonfungible tokens are blockchain-based tokens that each represent a unique asset like a piece of art, digital content, or media. Technically you own the rights to nothing but a piece of paper that says you own something. The profit potential mostly goes to the one selling.

32. Meditate, pray, relax after trading each day. I will mention it repeatedly, do not let trading control you. This is a non-emotional approach you need to take when trading. It is buy, sell, go about your day loving what you are doing.

Golden Rules for Losing Traders (found on the Internet, author unknown, but spot on):

1. Always add to a losing trade by averaging down. It will come back up eventually.
2. Always risk at least 25% of your trading capital on every trade to make the big bucks. A grand slam is better than a single.
3. Trade anything that looks good, even if you do not understand it.
4. Trade against the trend because you are smarter than the market.
5. Try to hit it out of the park with low probability, high risk-reward setups. You only need one good signal to make it worth the risk.
6. Ignore your plan, your system, your signals, the chart, and price action. Follow your opinions, bias, or predictions. If it feels good, do it.
7. Copy someone else's trading methodology because they are just like you.
8. Trade before you have a complete trading plan, even if you have no rules on entries, exits, and risk management. Strike while the iron is hot.
9. The size of your wins and losses does not matter if you are lucky.

10. Your risk management rules have nothing to do with the success of your technical trading system. If you are right this time, you will usually be right.

Special Note on Trading Triple-Leveraged ETFs

Triple-leveraged ETFs are not designed to be traded for extended periods of time because of the decay in holding them as we have shown. Leveraged ETFs are not designed for swing trading in most cases, however, there is opportunity to catch a few weeks trend. Before trading leveraged ETFs, you must first know the rules forwards and backwards and prove to yourself you can trade profitably with a disciplined plan on a consistent basis. This is necessary before you start taking on the added risk of trading leveraged ETFs.

Trading Rules Wrap-Up

If you do well in trading, give back to your Church or community or whatever your passion is. See what you can do to make a difference in this world. Share your success with others.

Briefly, these trading rules dictate the following major theme: *have a plan, trade your plan, keep stops and take profit.*

Chapter 14 - Trading Strategies

Glossary of terms—if there is a word you do not understand, do look it up in this glossary from stockcharts.com (see link below), or Google the term with the word "Investopedia."[104]

Many of the definitions below are either from Investopedia or thinkorswim software.

Trading For Profit

Mind-Set Ground Rules

There are many types of traders, and you must decide what type of trader you are as you go through the various strategies to trade. In the pages that follow, you will be able to do that. You will know if you are a day trader and have the time to sit in front of a computer and trade with the markets or a swing trader that can follow a trading plan they can profit from while going about their work and lives. I personally prefer to have a life and thus have built my trading system around swing trading but you'll also learn in this chapter some good setups for day trades.

Both types of trading require you to be hands-on and active with your trading. If you take the steps in this book to trade the markets, have a plan, and execute the plan based on the strategies provided, you will succeed in trading. You will find that being proactive with managing your wealth is better than being a passive investor. You will also decide if trading is something for you or if a professional manager is the route you should go. I want you to succeed as a trader, following the rules and I am providing you with the tools necessary to do so.

The old days of trading you needed a few desktop monitors to look at data and charts and decide on what to buy before trading. You

---

[104] https://school.stockcharts.com/doku.php?id=glossary_a

can do that from a cell phone or laptop while having lunch today. But the real homework is done each night after the market closes in preparation for the next trading day.

It is imperative when day trading and swing trading that you have your cell phone with you when away from your desktop and an app to trade from with your present online broker. News can come at any time that can be important for your positions.

Market hours are as follows: The New York Stock Exchange (NYSE) and Nasdaq, two major U.S. stock exchanges, typically trade Monday through Friday from 9:30 AM to 4 PM Eastern Time (ET). However, investors can buy and sell stocks outside of these hours through pre-market and after-hours trading. Pre-market trading can begin as early as 4 AM ET, and after-hours trading can last until 8 PM ET. During these times, buyers and sellers can interact directly on electronic communication networks (ECNs).

Interactive Brokers and Robinhood start trading at 1:00am but have made it a 24-hour tradeable market recently. However, one must be careful trading these hours as spreads can be wide and volatility higher. Most brokers begin trading at 4:00am. Liquidity is low during those first 2/12 hours before the market opens but for some, it is an advantage to trade pre-market or post-market, especially if you need to get out of a trade because of news.

Day Trader Versus Swing Trader

A day trader gets into a trade and can either stay for seconds, minutes, hours, and even a few days if the momentum, charts, and trend dictate it. Many day traders get in and get out of a trade and go home flat with no open positions at the end of the trading day. They do not take the risk of what news can do to their trade overnight and are always in control. Tomorrow is a new day and new opportunities for them.

Day traders typically trade the 1 minute and 5 minutes charts looking for good entries and exits based on the signals you will read about later in this book. Traders of triple-leveraged ETFs are mostly day traders.

Day traders follow the symbol /ES for trading S&P 500 futures to follow market trends to determine if they want to go long or short the market. They simply follow the trend up or down and take profits along the way letting some of the remaining trade capture the potential of a bigger move higher.

A day trader can range from scalping for dollars buying and selling quickly or going for bigger profit if the momentum in the chart is in their favor, at least or until they sell half shares to lock in profit or hit a resistance area based on one of the trading strategies you'll learn soon.

Swing traders look for multiday, week, or month or even longer trades that follow a trend. They are more concerned with the hourly and daily charts and breakouts to go along with the trend. They do not scalp for quick profits but go for a bigger return. You will learn what exit strategies for swing trades can be utilized to maximize profits. I have spent 4 years diligently researching this aspect of trading as it is the most important. Many traders will buy and hold and be in a huge profit only to see the stock reverse direction as they are clueless as to when to sell.

The key to swing trading is to have as many trades as possible going to diversify your risk while also leaving some cash set aside for future trades. You do not always have to be fully invested. Eventually there will be sell signals to take profit and free up cash as you wait for the next trade. Some trades will be losers and you must know when to cut losses or just ride them until they become profitable if the trend is still with you. You can combine much of what you learn in the coming chapters to know the best setups for buying and selling. I try to make this simple for you, but diversification is key to your success.

Obviously the larger the account, the more trades you can have working at the same time. But you must be able to manage each trade separately. You must be able to spend the time each day preparing for the next day's price action on whether to continue to hold or make other adjustments. While my trading service offers clear entry and exit strategies, you can make up your own mind when to take profit as well. The saying "always be taking profits" is the best motto to have.

Do not start your first attempts at trading by starting with the leveraged ETFs no matter what the size of your account. If you do finally work up to leveraged ETFs, start with the smaller trades into them first with just 1/100 of your account and work your way up to bigger trades after some profitable investment experiences. The moves in leveraged ETFs can be fast and wicked at times and are not for the novice. For example, leveraged trading in natural gas they nickname "the widow maker" simply because the price can move from Friday close to Monday opening 20% or more. The last thing you want to do as an investor is blow up your account with triple leverages investments. For a day trade now and then, I will provide some good setups to trade, but again, I do not recommend trading leveraged ETFs.

Both day and swing traders should become familiar with the trading software they are using. If day trading, you need to know what a level 2 screen is as that reveals the bid and the ask and market depth of each trade you make. Below is a sample. You buy on the ask (right side) and sell on the bid (left side). Level 2 is necessary for your trading so you know in a moving market where to place your buy and sell orders.

Trading Strategies

I want to start off this Trading Strategies section with an overview first. That overview is provided by a CFA (Chartered Financial Analyst) David Brady, who used to run a trading site and someone I have learned from over the years and have benefitted from the expertise he shares. He is especially good at giving traders the big picture. From there I will break-down the various strategies with other experts I have learned from over the years and wrap it up with what I think will work for you in setting up your own accounts to trade and what to look for so you can find easier roads to profit rather than trying to figure all this out yourself.

It has taken me twenty-five years of trading and a total of 38 years in the financial services industry to put the pieces of the puzzle together on what works and what does not when investing for the future. I have made every mistake one can make investing and you can learn from these mistakes, so you do not repeat them.

Remember, this section can be used for both day and swing traders, but for leveraged ETFs you must be quicker with stops and taking profit as a day trader. You will find that by following these strategies you will see how your account can grow year after year with some discipline, a strategy (plan), and an exit strategy if for any reason the trade does not work out.

The Holistic Approach to Trading vs the Purist's Approach by David Brady, CFA

Sentiment, COT positioning, technicals, EWT (Elliott Wave Theory), Fibonacci's, inter-market analysis, fundamentals, and trend following are used widely. There will always be those who say this is better than that, purists I call them, but I disagree. Obviously, each of them has merit because so many traders use them and yet each of the tools can be wrong at times. Hence, why I use all of them, and when they all say the same thing, you can have a high degree of confidence in your view. When they contradict each other you can either sit and wait for the right entry or hedge your position. I have evaluated this approach for over twenty years, and it works extremely well.

The purists with respect to one or the other tool always come out and scream, "See, this is the only method to use" when their tool is working, and others are not. But they are only doing it at that point in time because their tool was not working beforehand, and the others were. They focus on the moment, not performance over time. The truth is they all have their strengths and weaknesses, and this is why I prefer to use them all in combination with one another. Let me explain.

Sentiment (DSI) Daily Sentiment Index—This is a contrarian tool and works in all environments, trending or choppy, but it excels in choppy markets, for example, Gold 2016–2019. It is a "short-term" indicator, meaning that, at extremes, it signals a move in the opposite direction is coming. In choppy markets, it is excellent at calling peaks and troughs, especially in conjunction with other tools like technicals and COT positioning. In trending markets like the rally in Gold from 2001 to 2011 or the decline from 2011 to 2015, it still works extremely well at calling the ST peaks and troughs along the way.

Contrary to the delusions of the crowd, trending markets do not go straight up or down, they have short-term pullbacks and dead cat bounces all along the way up or down. The DSI data (discussed later) for the periods mentioned clearly prove this. The only difference in a trending market is that you must adjust how you use DSI. In choppy markets, DSI tends to go from ten to ninety and back again. In an uptrend, it goes from fifty to ninety and back again. In a downward trending market, it goes from ten to fifty and back again. As always, never use this in isolation or any tool for that matter.

Could it signal an extreme bullish market for weeks or months and the market does not fall, such as in an upward trending market? Sure, but eventually the market does fall, either in a ST pullback or a violent sell-off. DSI numbers in WTI (oil) over the past three years are perfect examples of this. But the notion that this tool no longer works is akin to the "this time is different" logic; it is never different. Sentiment, as behavioral finance shows, will always work because it exposes the delusion of the crowds at extremes, extremes that can be exploited for profitable trading or investment purposes.

COT Positioning—This works similarly to sentiment; it is best at extremes. When the large speculators aka "Specs" aka non-commercials (dumb money) are extremely long or short and the smart money banks or commercials are extremely short or long, 90% of the time, the market goes down or up respectively. All you must do is run a chart on the price of any asset against either specs or commercials to illustrate this is true, going back decades. But positioning, like sentiment, is a short-term tool, meaning, it indicates peaks and troughs in the short term, which works best in choppy markets but also in trending markets, if to a lesser extent. This is why Specs can remain long for a while and the market keeps going up in an upward trending market, the same when they are short in a downward trending market, but ultimately those markets will reverse as positioning and sentiment reverse. Again, the idea that these tools do not work suddenly after a breakout despite having worked for decades previous where numerous other such breakouts occurred is just plain silly and reveals bias on the part of the proponent. Bias clouds judgment.

Technical Indicators—Highs, lows, momentum, divergences, overbought, oversold, channels, flags, and so on work in all timeframes based on which chart you use hourly, daily vs weekly, or monthly. An asset can remain extremely overbought hourly, daily, and even weekly in an upward trending market, but when it is overbought on all timeframes, it capitulates, as the S&P showed in Oct 2018. The same goes for when it is oversold. Like sentiment and COT positioning, technical' s work best at extremes and can also signal peaks and troughs in choppy markets and in the short-term in both upward and downward trending markets. The merit in technicals is displayed by the fact that all professional traders use them. Do technicals cease to work because of a breakout? Of course not. No tool does.

Using these three tools together can also signal major turning points in trending markets, that is, when trends end or begin.

Elliott Waves and Fibonacci's—The strength of these tools is that they are based on market sentiment, like the DSI, but can be used to determine the short-, medium-, long-, and very long-term direction of the markets. They ignore what everything else is saying and rely solely on Fibonacci's work and wave counts. In that sense, they are a perfect complement to the other tools. The downside to this method is that it is subjective in nature and wave counts can move from one minute to the next based on the change in price. Hence why it works best in conjunction with other tools—sensing a theme yet?

Inter-market Analysis—This refers to the relationship between different assets and how the performance in one can affect another. For example, it is no secret that the dollar and gold often go in opposite directions as do real yields and gold. Therefore, we can gauge the next direction of gold based on our analysis of bigger markets like FX and bonds. The dog wags its tail, not the other way around. Now correlations come and go and there are even episodes where gold and the dollar and real yields all head in the same direction, hence the need to use this tool in combination with others. But when all these tools say the same thing, the message is powerful.

Fundamentals—Fundamentals provide the big picture. Despite what the behavioralists, technicians, and Elliotticians say, the fundamentals provide the big picture for what is going to happen to assets in the long term and can be catalysts for moves in the short term. Nonfarm payrolls may have minor impact on assets in the long term, but it sure does move markets in the short term. Should the Fed decide to revert to QE (quantitative easing) and MMT (modern monetary theory), I do not need any other tool to tell me that risk assets like stocks are likely to go up significantly and inflation-hedging assets like gold and silver also. It does not matter what kind of market we are in; fundamentals are always important IMHO. Anyone suggesting the opposite is ignoring history and reality.

Trend Following—Trend following works best when there is a definitive trend, as we saw in gold from 2001 to 2011 and 2011 to 2015 and the S&P from 2009 to 2019. However, trying to follow trends in choppy markets like that in gold since 2016 and the DXY (Dollar Index) since 2016 could get you killed financially. Just when you get a higher low and higher high, you go long and it breaks the prior low, and then you get a lower high and a lower low, and go short, and it breaks to a higher high. Trend following is price chasing by definition. You are late to the game in that you must wait for confirmation with a higher high, followed by higher low and another higher high, and vice versa on the downside, but could get caught heavily long or short when the tide decides to turn suddenly in the opposite direction. Refer to the choppy markets I mentioned earlier. No professional trader does this in isolation. But when the trend pays off by continuing over months or even years and you use trailing stops to capture all the move, you can get paid handsomely or even become rich on one strong trend move. But the idea that you can just blindly follow a trend in a vacuum is ludicrous to say the least, and anyone who suggests as much is just revealing their ignorance of how markets really work.

I hope this helps you understand why having an appreciation for all tools, knowing their strengths and weaknesses, and using them all in combination with one another works so well and why none of them ever lose their merit. Purists that suggest the contrary are simply speaking out of bias, the human weakness which destroys portfolios primarily. It may take more time to use this holistic approach, but the reward of doing so justifies the work put in.

To summarize, wait for near-perfect setups and then trade those, that is, extremes in technicals, sentiment, and COT positioning all at the same time. It is called a FIPTEST: Fundamentals, Inter-market analysis, Positioning, Trend Following, Elliott Waves (Fibonacci levels), Sentiment, and Technical Analysis (Classical) all have merit. Use them all when they agree and load up!

Let us dive into each of these separately.

Daily Sentiment Index (DSI)

The Daily Sentiment Index is offered up by Jake Bernstein, and it is used for pinpointing market turns.[105] It is a service you must pay for, but if you are a serious trader, and already profiting well, it is worth the extra expense. Below are the links to check it out. However, through some of the trading chat rooms you might ask who has DSI data and find it either delayed or for free. See the footnote to this sentence for a 2 hour video describing DSI.[106]

Bernstein's conclusions:

Daily Sentiment Index at extremes: Typical behavior in gathering over eighteen years of daily sentiment several clear patterns have emerged. They are as follows:

- When the DSI rises to the eighty-five area or higher the odds of a top are significant.
- When the DSI falls to the fifteen area or lower, the odds of a bottom are significant.
- The longer the DSI remains at an elevated level, the larger and longer the coming decline is likely to be
- The longer the DSI remains at a low level, the larger and longer the coming rally is likely to be.

---

[105] https://www.trade-futures.com/dsireport.php
[106] http://trade-futures.com/PINPOINTMARKETTURNS/PINPOINTMARKETTURNS.html

- The small trader is not always wrong at turning points, they are usually wrong at extremes.
- The DSI can be used as a timing indicator on its own.
- The DSI can be used as a timing indicator when combined with other indicators and as part of an overall trading model.

The nutshell synopsis here says to start looking long once it gets to fifteen or below and sell when eighty-five or higher.

You can see in the following table how certain asset classes move over time. Notice for example, from right to left, T-bonds were at the 80–93 level and on the following four trading days the level fell to the 53–75 level. Shorting T-bonds would have been a good trade.

SAMPLE	Network Press Inc., Daily Sentiment Index																								
DSI	08-19					08-16					08-15					08-14					08-13				
T-Bonds	53	56	70	77	75	45	68	77	80	77	71	84	86	84	79	87	90	87	86	80	93	91	87	85	80
S&P Index	71	70	64	59	46	68	69	62	55	45	71	61	60	49	42	68	57	58	43	38	44	54	51	40	35
Nasdaq Index	71	69	61	53	44	69	57	65	48	41	68	56	61	42	38	66	47	47	37	34	32	40	41	32	31
Dollar Index	55	37	34	40	46	26	27	30	40	43	28	29	34	44	45	25	31	40	44	44	33	39	44	47	43
Crude Light	89	86	82	65	64	85	82	79	62	63	65	70	59	61		77	76	59	57	60	75	62	50	55	60
Natural Gas	77	74	70	58	55	75	70	68	53	55	71	66	61	48	52	65	65	55	45	51	63	56	47	43	50
Gold	16	23	26	44	34	25	26	35	48	34	28	32	44	49	33	24	41	51	51	35	45	56	61	51	39
Silver	15	20	22	32	24	23	21	26	33	24	22	24	31	34	23	19	28	36	34	26	30	39	41	34	28
Copper	43	43	34	27	25	41	35	29	24	23	45	28	25	22	21	19	20	20	19	20	20	21	19	21	20
Corn	79	81	85	80	73	81	86	88	80	73	86	96	86	80	72	92	91	82	79	72	52	84	78	76	71
Wheat	77	75	81	82	74	73	78	83	82	73	75	84	84	83	73	86	86	85	83	73	92	87	85	81	73
Oats	76	77	80	75	70	75	80	80	75	69	80	83	79	74	69	84	82	76	73	69	85	76	73	71	69
Soybean	61	72	78	74	67	73	80	82	73	68	82	85	80	75	67	85	86	75	74	68	87	78	73	73	67
Coffee	12	14	17	18	17	15	18	19	18	18	15	20	28	19	18	24	22	21	19	17	20	20	19	16	17
Cocoa	73	71	58	62	62	69	69	64	60	61	72	66	62	57	60	65	60	58	53	61	62	57	57	53	62
Sugar	45	57	59	60	57	60	63	61	61	58	67	63	61	60	59	63	59	61	59	59	60	59	61	58	60
Lumber	23	21	20	19	22	19	19	19	19	22	21	20	19	22		18	18	19	21	21	22	19	18	23	21
CRB Index	72	77	78	71	66	77	80	79	69	64	82	80	76	67	63	80	79	71	65	64	79	73	66	63	64
Nikkei Index	29	30	28	28	23	28	30	27	27	23	33	28	28	26	23	28	24	27	24	22	24	26	27	22	21

* = Market Closed | Copyright © 2019, Jake Bernstein

At the end of each of these sections, you will be able to summarize that when everything is lined up that corresponds with a low DSI number, the time is nigh for buying and vice versa for selling when the DSI number is high. The best DSI number to look for is in the single digits (under ten) at extremes or 90's to consider selling or going short. But always keep to your trading plan as Bernstein warns in another video that sentiment can stay in the extreme for a long time. The longer sentiment stays in the extreme however, the more powerful the next move up or down becomes. The good news is, we have our other indicators to help guide us as to timing of our entry.

https://www.youtube.com/watch?v=SEobocGSVF4

Who uses DSI? DSI is used by some of the most well-known institutional investors, money managers, banks, and brokerage firms the world over and is available for individual traders too.

COT Positioning

I have found David Brady one of the best experts on COT positioning so this section is from him.

We primarily use COT positioning for trading gold and silver as it is a great asset for day and swing traders, but also can be used for going long or short natural gas another great asset to trade.

Gold: trading COT reports and dumb money I trade against the so-called dumb money, the funds or money managers. They always tend to be wrong at extremes.

High open interest is a secondary indicator of over bullishness and low open interest or lack of interest, that is, bearishness. It is that simple at the end of the day. There are other things I look at such as how fast they increase or reduce their positions, but that is it. Nothing complicated.

Positioning: Gold Funds

- Okay, another major tool I use in addition to technicals is positioning provided by the Commitment of Traders or COT Report.
- This shows how the bullion banks, the smart money and usually right, and hedge funds, the dumb money and usually wrong, are positioned.
- What we can gauge from this is if the hedge funds are über-long and the banks are extremely short, then gold is likely to fall, as the smart money is usually right and the dumb money is usually wrong.
- And the opposite is true too. Gold is likely to rise if the hedge funds are short and banks are long, or both are close to neutral.
- Focusing on just the hedge funds, or dumb money positioning, we can see in the next chart that gold prices bottomed in Dec.15 when funds were short, peaked in July16 when funds were record long, bottomed again when funds had reduced their longs to near zero, and then recently peaked again in, you guessed it mid-April.

- You can clearly see how extreme positioning by the hedge funds can signal a bottom or a peak is close.

Combine this information with what we will talk about next, and you can see how powerful these tools become when combined and how confident you can feel about trading or investing using them.

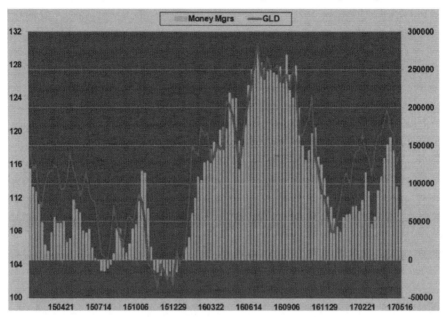

Where to find the COT data:

https://www.cftc.gov/MarketReports/CommitmentsofTraders/index.htm

https://www.dailyfx.com/forex/technical/ssi/xau-usd/2018/08/23/ssi_xau-usd.html

Thank you David Brady for your analysis. David runs a trading service called The FIPTEST Report focusing on gold and silver and miners you can find here:

https://fipestreport.substack.com/

Technical's: Bulk of Everything Investing

I am using the thinkorswim trading software from Schwab (formerly TD Ameritrade) for this section. You will have to set up an account with Schwab, who is my favorite broker because of their software, first and then follow a link they provide to download the trading software called thinkorswim. Interactive Brokers, Robinhood and Etrade are other brokers you can use. Not all of these brokerage houses are running 100% of the time so if you are in a trade and your broker's website crashes, make sure you have a second account to trade with and hedge your current trade until the broker's site is back up and running.

Some of the technical analysis and setups for this section I got from a fellow trader called Gelstretch and I thank him for his contribution over the years. He has explained these setups but primarily trades options off of them, which is beyond the scope of this book. We will discuss his thoughts on options in a bit, but it is best you learn the basics of trading first and conquer this kind of trading with the technicals before you enter the options world and the risk it involves.

I have listed these technical indicators alphabetically. Combining all you learn here should give you a full understanding not just of when to buy, but also when to sell. When you decide to lock in profit is up to you, but your goal is to lock some profit in as the trade moves higher leaving the rest to run if it wants to. Build your account first and get used to seeing it grow. Check your greed at the door and work on your trading plan.

Bollinger Bands

What is a Bollinger Band®? A Bollinger Band® is a technical analysis tool defined by a set of lines plotted with two standard deviations (positively and negatively) away from a simple moving average (SMA) of the security's price but can be adjusted to user preferences. Bollinger Bands® were developed and copyrighted by famous technical trader John Bollinger. There are three lines that compose Bollinger Bands: a simple moving average (middle band) and an upper and lower band.[107]

---

[107] https://www.investopedia.com/terms/b/bollingerbands.asp

Sample:

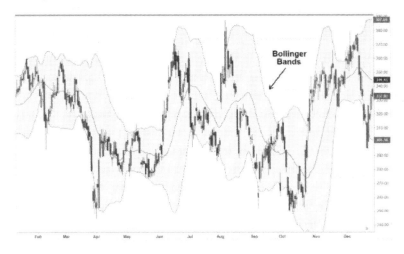

You can see as price gets to the top or bottom of the Bollinger Bands, reversals occur. The Bollinger Bands tighten when there is a squeeze in price going on and expand quickly when the breakout materializes, and price will follow the dominant band where you increase the investment size.

CCI (Commodity Channel Index)

Introduced by Donald Lambert, the Commodity Channel Index (CCI) was designed to identify cyclical turns in commodities but is now commonly applied to stock analysis. Its premise is that stocks move in cycles, with highs and lows forming at visually identifiable (yet ever-changing) periodic intervals. It is advised that one-third of the cycle length be used as a period for CCI. The CCI calculation can be applied to any indicator to determine the direction and strength of its trend.

CCI oscillates around zero. When CCI crosses up through +100, the indicator being analyzed is in an uptrend; when it crosses down through -100, the indicator is in a strong downtrend.[108]

---

[108] https://www.tc2000.com/help/Content/Indicators/
Commodity%20Channel%20Index.htm

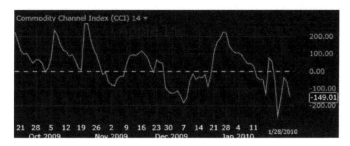

Students should watch for the CCI on the thirty-min bars of NUGT to turn positive. A positive turn would suggest that Wave 3 up is starting. Because NUGT is three times leveraged ETF, students might want to consider stepping into the trade using the CCI on the 30s and 60s as triggers.

DMI Oscillator

The directional movement indicator (also known as the directional movement index or DMI) is a valuable tool for assessing price direction and strength. It was created in 1978 by J. Welles Wilder, who also created the popular relative strength index (RSI). The DMI is especially useful for trend trading strategies because it differentiates between strong and weak trends, allowing the trader to enter only the ones with real momentum.[109]

Set it at 5 Exponential. A quick glance, and you know where price is likely to go... works on all timeframes.

Divergence Trading

Divergence is when the price of an asset is moving in the opposite direction of a technical indicator, such as an oscillator, or is moving contrary to other data. Divergence warns that the current price trend may be weakening and, in some cases, may lead to the price changing direction. There are positive and negative divergences. Positive divergence indicates a move higher in the price of the asset is possible. Negative divergence signals that a move lower in the asset is possible.[110]

---

[109] https://www.investopedia.com/articles/technical/02/050602.asp
[110] https://www.investopedia.com/terms/d/divergence.asp

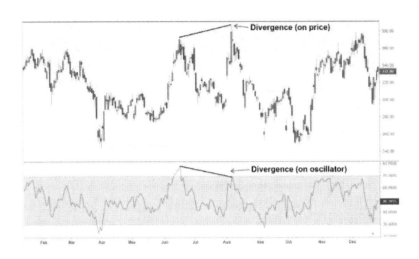

Higher Highs and Lower Lows

An effective way to trade is looking to trade breakouts. On a day when the market is moving higher, look for trades that are breaking the prior day's high. You are looking for a trend that has higher highs and higher lows. If the market is falling lower, look for the opposite. Look for lower lows and lower highs and short it.

Some days though you will not want to trade at all and those are called inside and outside days. On an inside day you will see a lower high and higher low and an outside day a higher high and lower low.

Ichimoku Cloud (preferred by Technical Analysis connoisseurs).

The Ichimoku Cloud is a collection of technical indicators that show support and resistance levels, as well as momentum and trend direction. It does this by taking multiple averages and plotting them on the chart. It also uses these figures to compute a "cloud" which attempts to forecast where the price may find support or resistance in the future.[111]

Keltner Channel

A Keltner channel is a volatility-based technical indicator composed of three separate lines. The middle line is an exponential

---

[111] https://www.investopedia.com/terms/i/ichimoku-cloud.asp

moving average (EMA) of the price. Additional lines are placed above and below the EMA. The upper band is typically set two times the average true range (ATR) above the EMA, and lower band is typically set two times the ATR below the EMA. The bands expand and contract as volatility (measured by ATR) expands and contracts. Since most price action will be encompassed within the upper and lower bands (the channel), moves outside the channel can signal trend changes or an acceleration of the trend. The direction of the channel, such as up, down, or sideways, can also aid in identifying the trend direction of the asset.[112]

VWAP Volume-Weighted Average Price

The volume-weighted average price (VWAP) is a technical analysis indicator used on intraday charts that resets at the start of every new trading session. It's the average price a security has traded at throughout the day, based on both volume and price.

MACD (Moving Average Convergence Divergence)

Moving Average Convergence Divergence (MACD) is a trend-following momentum indicator that shows the relationship between two moving averages of a security's price. The MACD is calculated by subtracting the twenty-six-period Exponential Moving Average (EMA)

112 https://www.investopedia.com/terms/k/keltnerchannel.asp

from the twelve-period EMA. The result of that calculation is the MACD line. A nine-day EMA of the MACD called the "signal line" is then plotted on top of the MACD line, which can function as a trigger for buy and sell signals. Traders may buy the security when the MACD crosses above its signal line and sell, or short, the security when the MACD crosses below the signal line. MACD indicators can be interpreted in several ways, but the more common methods are crossovers, divergences, and rapid rises/falls.[113]

McClellan Oscillator

What is the McClellan Oscillator? The McClellan Oscillator is a market breadth indicator that is based on the difference between the number of advancing and declining issues on a stock exchange, such as the New York Stock Exchange (NYSE) or NASDAQ. The indicator is compared to stock market indices related to the exchange. The indicator is used to show strong shifts in sentiment in the indices, called breadth thrusts. It also helps in analyzing the strength of an index trend via divergence or confirmation.[114]

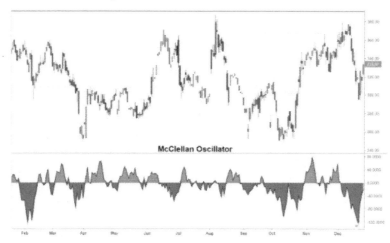

Money Flow Index

Money flow is calculated by averaging the high, low, and closing prices and multiplying by the daily volume. Comparing the results of

---

[113] https://www.investopedia.com/terms/m/macd.asp
[114] https://www.investopedia.com/terms/m/mcclellanoscillator.asp

that with the number from the previous day tells traders whether money flow was positive or negative for the current day. Positive money flow indicates that prices are likely to move higher, while negative money flow suggests prices are about to fall.

What is the Money Flow Index (MFI)? The MFI is a technical oscillator that uses price and volume for identifying overbought or oversold conditions in an asset. It can also be used to spot divergences which warn of a trend change in price. The oscillator moves between 0 and 100. Unlike conventional oscillators such as the Relative Strength Index (RSI), the Money Flow Index incorporates both price and volume data, as opposed to just price. For this reason, some analysts call MFI the volume-weighted RSI. The indicator is typically calculated using fourteen periods of data.[115]

An MFI reading above eighty is considered overbought, and an MFI reading below twenty is considered oversold. You can see in the chart below that each time the MFI went above eighty (encircled), the price eventually moved lower.

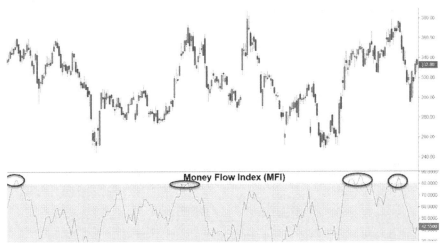

Money Flow Index (MFI)

Moving Averages

A moving average (MA) is a widely used indicator in technical analysis that helps smooth out price action by filtering out the "noise" from random short-term price fluctuations. It is a trend-

---

[115] https://www.investopedia.com/terms/m/mfi.asp

following, or lagging, indicator because it is based on past prices. The two basic and commonly used moving averages are the simple moving average (SMA), which is the simple average of a security over a defined number of time periods, and the exponential moving average (EMA), which gives greater weight to more recent prices.[116]

Exponential moving averages are best for triple leveraged because they move faster with price.

The 20 EMA is the most useful for trends. Price will rise to the 20 EMA, struggle there and maybe dip back down to the 8 EMA before rising again to 20 EMA, 50 EMA, and ultimately to the 200 EMA. If you have been long with the trend and eventually fall below the 50 EMA, whether or not you hit the 200 EMA first, the decline below the the "line in the sand" and a sign to exit the trade.

The hourly chart will dictate sentiment and major trend change if accompanied by an increase in volume. If there is a decrease in price after that first move up, with lower volume, then the setup is there for liftoff in price and confirmation of the direction of the trend.[117]

Price Patterns

Jesse Livermore did not have the ability to use charts on a computer to track price patterns but would do so on graph paper in front of him. Getting to know these patterns and how they repeat is what we try to profit from as investors. When you add pivot points to the mix, it gives us targets. What we look for breakouts and combined with the relative strength we talk about soon and the other indicators, we have permission to hold for more profit.

Pivot Points

Pivot points' purpose is to provide three key support and resistance levels using daily, weekly, or monthly timeframes. Support and resistance levels are found in relation to the pivot point which is the

---

[116] https://www.investopedia.com/terms/m/movingaverage.asp
[117] https://school.stockcharts.com/
doku.php?id=technical_indicators:moving_averages

average of High, Low, and Close prices of the previous period. See the following table explaining calculation of support and resistance levels.[118]

The formulas for pivot points:

The Formulas for Pivot Points:

$$P = \frac{\text{High} + \text{Low} + \text{Close}}{3}$$

$$R1 = (P \times 2) - \text{Low}$$

$$R2 = P + (\text{High} - \text{Low})$$

$$S1 = (P \times 2) - \text{High}$$

$$S2 = P - (\text{High} - \text{Low})$$

where:

$P = \text{Pivot point}$

$R1 = \text{Resistance 1}$

$R2 = \text{Resistance 2}$

$S1 = \text{Support 1}$

$S2 = \text{Support 2}$

Note that High indicates the high price from the prior trading day, Low indicates the price from the prior trading day, and Close indicates the closing price from the prior trading day.

Order	Resistance Level	Support Level
First	Above the pivot point, at the distance equal to that between the pivot point and the Low price of the previous period.	Below the pivot point, at the distance equal to that between the pivot point and the High price of the previous period.
Second	Above the pivot point, at the distance equal to the trading range of the previous period.	Below the pivot point, at the distance equal to the trading range of the previous period.
Third	Above the second resistance level, at the distance equal to the trading range of the previous period.	Below the second support level, at the distance equal to the trading range of the previous period.

We provide this pivot point calculator with the Profit in Up and Down Markets trading platform.

Parabolic SAR

The Parabolic SAR, or parabolic stop and reverse, is a popular indicator that is mainly used by traders to determine the future short-

---

[118] https://www.investopedia.com/terms/p/pivotpoint.asp

term momentum of a given asset. The Parabolic SAR (Stop and Reverse) technical indicator is a study for analyzing trending markets. When the price is in an uptrend, the SAR appears below the price and converges upward toward it. Similarly, on a downtrend, the SAR appears above the price and converges downward.[119]

Here you will see a slant down on the graph or a slant up. You want to trade that direction.

Put–Call Ratio

The put–call ratio is an indicator ratio that provides information about relative trading volumes of an underlying security's put options to its call options. The put–call ratio has long been viewed as an indicator of investor sentiment in the markets, where a substantial proportion of puts to calls indicates bearish sentiment and vice versa.[120]

The Put–Call Ratio you can find live with this footnote.[121]

Technically, as the Put–Call Ratio heads to .50, it becomes extremely bullish, and as it heads to 1.50, it becomes extremely bearish as you can see in the next chart. Just another tool you can use with all the others to confirm your trade. See the next graph.

Use this footnote/endnote for the thinkorswim trading platform as a setup for the Put–Call Ratio.[122]

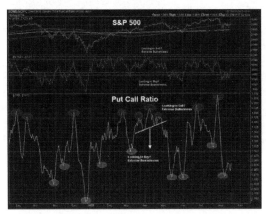

---

[119] https://www.investopedia.com/ask/answers/06/parabolicsar.asp
[120] https://www.investopedia.com/terms/p/putcallratio.asp
[121] http://www.cboe.com/data/current-market-statistics/cboe-daily-market-statistics
[122] http://tos.mx/w1r7qM

Relative Strength

Relative strength is a measure of the price trend of a stock or other financial instruments compared to another stock, instrument, or industry. It is calculated by taking the price of one asset and dividing it by another.[123]

You are looking for accelerated revenue growth, EPS, ready to come out of a long base with increasing (two to four times average) volume (100k or more), price of $15 or more, and a huge, short interest. The RS line hitting a fifty-two-week high before price that is close to a fifty-two-week high is what you also want.

On the other side, you can short with an RS line hitting new lows and about to break below its 50 DMA with say an earnings miss. The RS line should be moving lower before price does.

For passive investors, Dorsey Wright Relative Strength Fund (DALI) may have low volume today, but it tries to invest based off relative strength, outperforming the S&P but also follows the S&P down if the market goes down.

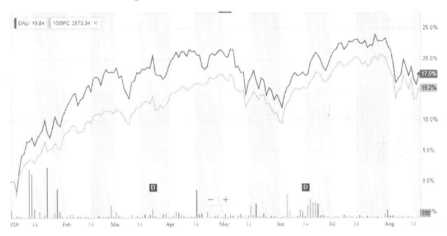

Relative Strength Index (RSI)

According to thinkorswim definitions section, the Relative Strength Index (RSI) is an oscillator that rates the strength of a security on a scale from 0 to 100, comparing magnitudes of its recent gains and losses. By default, the Wilder's moving average is used in

---

[123] https://www.investopedia.com/ask/answers/06/relativestrength.asp

the calculation of RSI for thinkorswim. RSI is widely used as an overbought/oversold indicator, with default values of thirty for the oversold level and seventy for the overbought.

RSI is used by many and by looking at the charts, you can see if it aligns with your other indicators for direction. A move below thirty indicates you can put the investment on your radar, and a move above seventy indicates you can start taking profit. Day traders will scalp with RSI on the one minute or five-minute chart, and swing traders will look for moving averages to coincide with the longer-term charts and stay in the investment longer for more profit.

Scanner

A scanner is found in thinkorswim. You can research it for yourself or use this link to get you started on finding the right trades with this footnote.[124]

Screening for Trades

Trading Gap Up and Gap Down

In thinkorswim, under the heading Marketwatch, go to Public (listed alphabetically) and select gap up or gap down. Stocks and ETFs that have made a big gap up typically will fill some of the gap lower after the open and become a buy. breaking to new highs. and vice versa if they gap down. Look at your other signals to see if they concur with the trend.

Stochastic Momentum Index (SMI)

According to thinkorswim definitions section, the Stochastic Momentum Index (SMI) is like the Stochastic Oscillator with the difference that it finds position of the Close price relative to the High-Low range's midpoint, not the range itself. This difference results in the oscillator being plotted on the -100 to +100 scale. It is considered a Buy signal when the SMI crosses above the oversold (-40) level and

---

[124] http://tos.mx/uEMkjX

a sell signal when it crosses below the overbought (+40) level. The primary plot is accompanied by its Exponential Moving Average so that additional signals are produced. Crossing above the EMA suggests the Buy signal; crossing below, Sell signal.

Tick Charts

According to thinkorswim definitions section, tick charts display a certain number of trades before printing a new bar and are often used by short-term traders. Unlike time-based charts, tick charts are based solely on the trading activity of each buy and sell transaction. Tick charts are commonly used by day traders who need to make quick trading decisions and do not have the time to wait for a three or a five-minute bar to close.

Gelstretch says some of the best intraday trading is done off the tick charts. The NYSE Tick indicator is a market breadth indicator used to determine short-term bullish or bearish market sentiment. It can be used for trading ES futures with the 987-tick setting. This is a real winner for anyone with the desire to make consistent returns and who has the time and concentration to devote to the task. My primary indicator is the DMI oscillator set at a length of five. For day traders, this one will pay the rent and all the vacations needed.

True Strength Index (TSI)

According to thinkorswim definitions section, the True Strength Index study is a variation of the Relative Strength Index (RSI). Unlike the RSI, this study uses double smoothing: a short average of a longer one. This type of smoothing is applied to both the one-bar momentum of the close price and its absolute value. The result is equal to the percentage ratio between the two values. Buy and Sell signals are indicated at crossovers of the primary plot with its average.

The TSI (10-3-10 setting) exponential and squeeze (discussed next) are two of the best signal sources to use, and I will quote Gelstretch on some of the explanation and guidance that follows.

TTM Squeeze

According to thinkorswim's definition section, the squeeze indicator measures the relationship between two studies: Bollinger Bands® and Keltner channels. When the volatility increases, so does the distance between the bands; conversely, when the volatility declines, the distance also decreases. The squeeze indicator finds sections of the Bollinger Bands® study which fall inside the Keltner channels. When the market finishes a move, the indicator turns off, which corresponds to bands having pushed well outside the range of Keltner channels. To produce Buy/Sell signals, the squeeze indicator is plotted along with momentum oscillator. The momentum oscillator histogram is smoothed up with linear regression and other techniques. When the indicator is on (green) and the momentum oscillator is colored cyan, it is considered a Buy signal (this signal is supposed to be correct until two blue bars in a row). When the indicator is on and the momentum oscillator is red, it is considered a Sell signal (this signal is supposed to be correct until two yellow bars in a row). When the indicator is off (red), no trade is recommended.

What you need are two consecutive yellow bars on the TTM squeeze (upward price momentum).

The squeeze is your signal of where price is headed. Trade the squeezes on the five- and fifteen-minute charts, and load the boat for these moves, but always have both timeframe charts up at the same time.

Gelstretch's mentor for learning how to trade the TTM squeeze is John Carter, and you can watch a twenty-five-minute video on it with this footnote.[125]

The squeeze is really a "momentum" indicator, and the change in color on the bars signals a change in momentum as the price waves roll in their typical pattern, thus effecting price.

Follow the squeezes not so much for price change, but more for the exponential expected moves in price, as the red dots on the zero-line change to the green dots and then price explodes directionally for seven to nine bars very quickly. If the squeeze is on a five-minute chart,

---

[125] https://www.youtube.com/watch?v=lbmUfauTGkU

then the breakout will last about forty-five minutes, which can give you a nice ride. If trading a squeeze on the daily chart, then you typically will get a seven-to-nine-day ride of consistent directional momentum. This happens about 75% of the time. The other 25% are momentum trades that may last only a few bars. I have found these indicators exceptionally important for trade timing— entries and exits that are often timed perfectly with confidence... and no guessing.

TTM Scalper Alert

According to thinkorswim's definition section, the TTM Scalper Alert is a great tool for runaway markets. Timing entry into a runaway market is haphazard at best and can be akin to stepping in front of a freight train. By waiting for a scalper alert to fire off, a trader can be sure that momentum has at least paused and allows an entry at a possible turning point with a precise risk/reward ratio in place. The TTM Scalper Alert comprises two plots, Pivot High and Pivot Low. Pivot High is shown as an arrow above the first bar in a series of three lower Closes (Sell signal). Pivot Low is shown as an arrow under the first bar in a series of three higher Closes (Buy signal).

Use the TTM Scalper Alert and RSI all in conjunction with one another. It helps improve the accuracy of direction confirmation.

Williams %R

According to thinkorswim's definition section, the Williams %R is a lower study. It is a momentum indicator that is designed to identify overbought and oversold areas in a non-trending market. The Williams %R can be interpreted similarly to the stochastic oscillators but the Williams %R is simply plotted upside down. Readings in the range of -80% to -100% may indicate that the security is oversold while readings in the 0% to -20% range suggest that it is overbought.

Elliott Waves and Fibonacci's

Ralph Nelson Elliott developed the Elliott Wave Theory in the 1930s. Elliott believed that stock markets, thought to behave in a random and chaotic manner, in fact traded in repetitive patterns. In this article, we will look at the history behind Elliott Wave Theory and how it is applied to trading. Elliott proposed that trends in financial prices resulted from investors' predominant psychology. He found that swings in mass psychology always showed up in the same recurring fractal patterns, or "waves," in financial markets. Elliott's theory resembles the Dow theory in that both recognize that stock prices move in waves. Because Elliott additionally recognized the "fractal" nature of markets, however, he was able to break down and analyze them in much greater detail. Fractals are mathematical structures, which on an ever-smaller scale infinitely repeat themselves. Elliott discovered stock index price patterns were structured in the same way. He then began to look at how these repeating patterns could be used as predictive indicators of future market moves.[126]

Let's have a look at the following chart made up of eight waves (five net up and three net down) labeled 1, 2, 3, 4, 5, A, B and C.

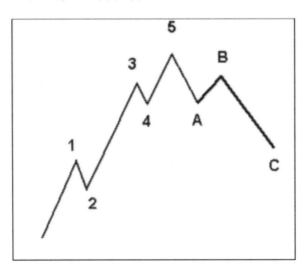

Waves 1, 2, 3, 4 and 5 form an impulse, and waves A, B and C form a correction. The five-wave impulse in turn forms wave 1 at the next-largest degree, and the three-wave correction forms wave 2 at the next-largest degree.

---

[126] https://www.investopedia.com/articles/technical/111401.asp

Elliott Wave counts are just road maps for targets. They are not exact, and they can and do morph into other wave counts. Many who make calls based on Elliott Wave typically take both sides of the market saying if the market goes up, then this wave count is valid, and if it goes down, the opposite. Elliott Wave should be used in conjunction with your other indicators.

There is someone who follows Elliott Wave better than anyone I know. His name is Avi Gilburt and he also has a trading service that uses Elliot Wave patterns. You can find him at the following link. https://www.elliottwavetrader.net/

Fibonacci

A Fibonacci retracement is a term used in technical analysis that refers to areas of support or resistance. Fibonacci retracement levels use horizontal lines to indicate where support and resistance levels are. Each level is associated with a percentage. The percentage is how much of a prior move the price has retraced. The Fibonacci retracement levels are 23.6%, 38.2%, 61.8%, and 78.6%. While not officially a Fibonacci ratio, 50% is also used. The indicator is useful because it can be drawn between any two significant price points, such as a high and a low, and then the indicator will create the levels between those two points.[127]

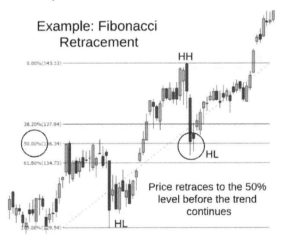

Chart from this footnote.[128]

---

[127] https://www.investopedia.com/terms/f/fibonacciretracement.asp
[128] https://thetrendtradingblog.com/2019/04/04/fibonacci-retracement/

Inter-Market Analysis

More from David Brady on Inter-Market Analysis: Many commodities work in reverse of the dollar or interest rates, dollar down, gold up, and interest rates up, gold down, for example. Looking for these correlations that are time tested can keep you in the trade a bit longer when used in conjunction with other indicators. It is not absolute, but I have followed the gold/dollar correlation (we showed that chart in the gold section) a long time, and it is one of the most consistent inverse trades I have seen.

Fundamentals

A different type of fundamental analysis has to do with market indicators that affect your trade. These are the economic indicators that come out each week from nonfarm payrolls to retail sales, manufacturing data, inflation data, GDP, unemployment rate, interest rates and so on. The data can also be specific to individual commodities like oil and natural gas storage. Knowing when these reports come out is important, especially for day traders. Sometimes if you are in good profit, you may want to sell and lock in profit before the data comes out.

You can find these indicators on investing.com at the footnote link and prepare your week accordingly. This will be provide with the trading service.[129]

Trend

The old saying "the trend is your friend" is one you always need to keep in the back of your mind. Another is "don't fight the trend." With all the indicators you have already been given, here are a few more to keep you on track.

Trend and the Fear and Greed Index—there is more in this link than just the following chart as it includes market volatility, put and call options, stock price strength, market momentum, stock price breadth, junk bond demand, and safe haven demand.

https://money.cnn.com/data/fear-and-greed/

---

[129] https://www.investing.com/economic-calendar/

Fear & Greed Index
What emotion is driving the market now?

Now:
Extreme
Fear

Previous Close
Extreme Fear 25

1 Week Ago
Extreme Fear 20

1 Month Ago
Greed 57

1 Year Ago
Greed 59

Next is a heat map. Are you trading against it or with it? The following chart was taken just after a -500 point down on Wall Street and a then President Trump tweet the market did not like related to tariffs on China. Before this tweet, the color on the Fear and Greed Index was all green and the markets were doing well. But market participants knew there was a Fed meeting at Jackson Hole, Wyoming and if President Trump did not get what he wanted out of Chair Powell, which he did not, he would of course tweet something about it, which he did. He doubled down with a retaliation tweet on additional China tariffs announced earlier in the day. You can watch the trend change by going to the footnote link. It is a good snapshot of the market at any time to see what is hot or not.[130]

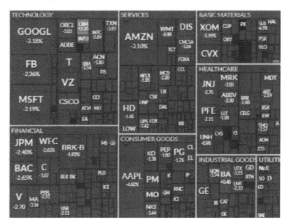

A more aggressive way to play a trend, for traders who have done their homework is based on techniques from a trader from Seeking

---

[130] https://www.finviz.com/

Alpha that I have followed over the years. This is not for new traders as there can be risk involved and should only be utilized with a small portion of your overall portfolio.

His comments below are related to trading in natural gas ETFs and other leveraged ETFs which have the most risk vs reward. Note that this section goes against my rules of adding to losing positions but it's worth mentioning for homework on a specific sector can pay off.

All these ETFs have their own conditions and market circumstances that affect when there is a perceived inflection point. If I were to lay out criteria, I would say:

1. An ETF has become grossly overbought or oversold.
2. The fundamentals do not support the price direction in #1 above.
3. The price movement took place because of some temporary market condition that fundamentals do not support.
4. Sentiment way to high without support of fundamentals.
5. Too much investment on one side of the trade.
6. Having market awareness of surrounding circumstances that legitimately could change price direction.
7. When many conditions exist above, use key support/resistance levels to add to your position.

The strategy is to keep adding to a position as it falls because fundamentals do not line up with price. It is this adding to your position part that can get a trader into trouble sometimes and you want to try and avoid putting all your eggs in one basket. For example, some ETFs are not suitable for this strategy, like UVIX (2x the volatility) as it doesn't line up with the markets. The last thing you want to do is blow up your account. Also, you never want to use this strategy with any margin/leverage.

A large part of knowing when to build a position comes from being plugged into the market and knowing the asset you are trading inside and out and what affects the price action. Waiting for the right time to begin the trade is crucial of course and that's where things like RSI and DSI come into play. Picking the correct inflection point is the key to success otherwise the potential for exceptionally large losses becomes greater.

If you build a position after something has been overbought or oversold, you have less risk of price action continuing against you. I look at using price action, fundamentals, and charts. Usually, I try and look ahead three or four months as that offers enough time to ensure you get the correct inflection point setup.

But I will say it is mentally draining watching your money go up, down, and all around while waiting for the larger move. Most would book profits or losses too early to benefit and get out before the bigger move comes.

If you analyze your trade history and objectively see what would have happened if you held that position longer rather than sell and buy back again a bunch of times, you can find yourself getting a bigger profit.

I am not saying anyone should hold everything all the time, because there's times when there is no clear fundamental direction. In this case day trading until a good setup comes along is fine. But you should be looking for those overbought or oversold conditions that do not line up with the fundamental picture to begin building a position for a longer-term hold.

I recommend everyone to regularly analyze your trading patterns as it can shed light on your weaknesses. I put all my trades in an Excel spreadsheet and use pivot tables and other tools to manipulate the information for thorough analysis.

You must be prepared that the losses will be larger, but the profits will be larger. It is imperative that you consistently execute your trades and formulate your analysis on the same fundamental approach. A long time ago, I analyzed all the ETFs I want to trade and decided on which fundamentals most directly affect the price movements for those ETFs. Then going forward, that is all you use to make your decisions for buying, selling, or holding. Not that you completely ignore everything else, but you do not let it influence your decisions.

Many go out searching for consensus to validate holding their underwater positions. In doing this you will be biased and read mostly articles that support your position, and even if you read the ones that do not, you will not take heed of that warning as it does not support your current trade. The key to success is the consistency behind how you execute your investments. You will notice I do not let anyone influence whether I buy or sell, not even the biggest of experts in their sector.

CHAPTER 15 - RETIREMENT

Let's face it, many of you are reading this book and learning what to trade to take more control of your future investments. Visa would rather you "be everywhere you want to be" and spend your money now, and their subliminal commercials are good at getting you to do that, rather than put away for your future retirement. Gone are the days of forced savings or defined benefit plans that take care of your retirement, unless of course you work for the government. But even if you work for the government, you better be doing some investing on your own.

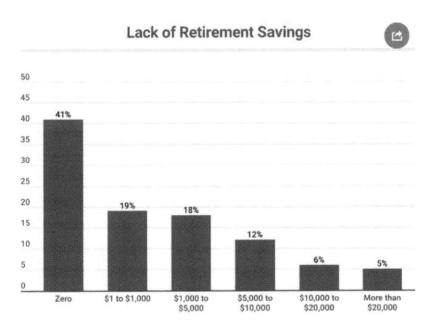

Lack of Retirement Savings

Seventy-nine percent of workers are offered a 401k to invest in, but only 41% of those utilize it which means that only 32% of the total workforce are saving for retirement.[131] We need to do something about this and hopefully you are on your way to increase those

---

[131] https://www.fool.com/retirement/2017/06/19/does-the-average-american-have-a-401k.aspx

numbers by taking out a 401k at work, especially if your company offers any matching of your contributions to go with it.

A recent Department of Labor and Statistics study on retirement revealed that US workers retiring in the 2050s will have saved enough in their 401(k) accounts to replace an average of only 22% of their preretirement income and 37% have no savings at all.[132] That is scary, but after reading this book, you can do something about it. Whether you are just getting into investing or already in retirement and holding on to what you have worked so hard for, you'll need to be proactive in managing your investments. If you do have a nest egg you have built, practice some investing that keeps you on the right side of the trend at all times, rather than experience any potential downturns that come.

While there are options for those who have a decent nest egg and a decent stream of income for retirement, like living in countries where the cost of living is much less, most would prefer to have enough wealth to stay at home and be near family and simply enjoy retirement. Retirement can still be fun and exciting with plenty of income as you will see. I do not want you to give up hope! Of course, if you are younger, you will build your retirement nest egg and be prepared no matter what the market does.

My favorite saying is, I don't care what the market does as long as I am on the right side of it. That is a better saying than your typical buy and hold strategy or as some might call it, buy and hope.

---

[132] https://www.census.gov/hhes/www/laborfor/Working-Beyond-Retirement-Age.pdf

PART 3 - RETIREMENT

CHAPTER 16 - SOCIAL SECURITY

Many who have contributed to the Social Security System calculate what they have paid into it over the years and compare what Social Security says they will receive to what they could have earned if they had done the investing themselves. But one thing is typically missing from this calculation. The employer also contributed to the social security pot an equal amount on their behalf. That amount is 6.2%, matching what you put in, or 12.4% in total.[133] Wouldn't you have rather received that extra 12.4% and invested it yourself, and have control of your investments so you could leave that wealth to your heirs if you didn't spend it all?

Many reading this might say that Social Security is there for those who need it most—the people who live off this income as their only means of support. I understand this, and do not deny it is an issue— an excessively big issue to many. And it will become more of an issue as seniors fight to make ends meet in the years to come as inflation kicks in. Social Security alone may not keep up with inflation, and most will not have put enough away to take care of themselves in their golden years. That is why it is important for you to take what you have learned from this book and invest accordingly.

Unfortunately, if you are younger, there may not be any social security for you, so you will have to invest even smarter to overcome that. You may be paying into a system that will in return give you nothing, but that is the subject of a future book called We the Serfs! Take what you learn here and treat your investing with a sincere effort rather than a passive one as the more you can have your wealth compound over the years starting at an early age, the better off you will be. Teach your children how investing early is the key for their

---

[133] http://www.irs.gov/taxtopics/tc751.html

future. Give them this book as a starting point. No one else is teaching them what to do to take care of themselves.

CHAPTER 17 - THE ILLUSION OF RETIRING AT SIXTY-FIVE

Many of us have been told that "you work your entire life, save up enough money, and then retire at age sixty-five." They say that with a Social Security supplement and your company pension plan, your retirement will be "golden." In your golden years it is supposed to be a life full of leisure.

A Nielsen survey showed that 69% of global respondents will achieve financial goals but only 28% think current planning efforts will be sufficient.[134] Americans believe in the fairy tale that if one works hard and invests their money wisely, by the time retirement comes, they will be set for life. But there are a few things that have changed since the days when the man typically brought home the bacon and the women stayed home with the kids. It now takes two incomes to maintain the same lifestyle as back then and you can blame that on inflation.

Your investments need to keep pace with inflation and more importantly, your wealth needs to maintain its purchasing power.

Spending Too Much and Saving Too Little

Part of the problem is that Americans are spending too much and saving far too little.[135]

One thing everyone saving for retirement must do is lose their "keep up with the Jones'" mentality. Your future retirement nest egg is more important than a new car to keep up with your neighbor—who is also struggling with their future of retirement. Managing credit card debt is what many are dealing with, and they must get that under control, too. The best thing to do is simply to cut down on credit cards and only use your debit cards while also curtailing your

---

[134] http://www.nielsen.com/us/en/press-room/2014/nielsen-survey-69-of-global-respondents-believe-they-will-achieve-financial-goals.html

[135] https://www.ici.org/pdf/2015_factbook.pdf

spending habits. No one else is going to provide for your retirement. It is up to you to work hard, earn an income, and invest wisely what you do manage to save. If it takes getting a second job to eliminate debt, then do it. Once someone maxes out their credit cards with high interest rates and pays the minimum payment each month, it is a never-ending debt that you cannot get rid of. The minimum payments could be going into investments but because of poor choices, they go into the pockets of the banks who provide the credit cards. Your first goal in investing is to have no debt. This way money works for you and not against you.

Younger generations are living in their parents' home longer, as it is difficult to afford to live on their own. This puts even more burden on the parents, who are trying to save for retirement—31% of millennials who make up the eighteen to thirty-one age brackets live with their parents.

If your kids are sponging off you, teach them what it takes to be successful and the fulfillment they will get by achieving wealth on their own. If they are sitting around playing video games, instead instruct them to do some simulated stock trading and get them motivated to have money working for them once they find work. You do not want them returning, keeping you from your retirement goals. We just cannot give handouts to children. They need to get to the point where they can take the wealth they have earned and utilize what is written in this book and grow it.

Retirement Plan Not Available or Limited to 401(k) with High Fees and No Options to Counter Declining Market

One reason retirement is an illusion for many is the ending of the defined benefit pension plans of the past, wherein the company you worked for promised you (and your spouse) an income that you couldn't outlive. This is what many retirees are living off of today, but many do not have the same options for retirement plans at work their parents had. Thirty-seven percent of the elderly in the United States collect pensions, but only 10% of baby boomers do.[136]

---

[136] http://finance.yahoo.com/news/baby-boomers—poorer-in-old-age-than-their-parents-162653066.html

Twenty million boomers are already entering retirement with a net worth of $50,000 or less, according to the Employee Benefit Research Institute (EBRI). Social Security is all they have for income.[137]

When you add in the recession that killed the lifeblood of savings in stocks that boomers had at that time, or factor in future potential recessions or worse, many may have to delay retirement if they are invested in such a way that the next downturn wipes out a good chunk of their retirement savings.

Boomers' only option for retirement are IRA's and a company's 401(k) plan and hope that these and additional investments are sufficient to meet their needs once retired.

After retiring, investors hope that they manage their funds to where they can afford to withdraw the percentage of their wealth, they need to maintain a comfortable retirement. This did not work so well in 2007–2009, when we saw many employees' 401(k)s lose a good percentage of their value. We did bounce back nicely for the next 13 years, but who is to say this will not happen again? How are investors prepared? Why do you as an investor want to ride a market lower when you do not have to?

Even those who invest in 401(k)s are not aware of all the fees involved when they look at the monthly statement (if they look at all). Many investment houses have gotten rich off the 401(k) investor, and if your company is still only providing you with a choice of high-fee mutual funds, then employees need to demand change. Last year alone, Wall Street bagged $17 billion in fees that went to advisors and plan administrators.[138] A simple no load index fund outperformed these mutual funds and those fees could be in investors accounts instead.

The investment choices for the 401(k)s employees have at work are also limited in options and typically have none of the inverse ETFs and funds we discussed in this book that allow an investor to profit from a falling market or at least hedge their portfolio. These investment choices for a 401k are limited to stocks, typically the S&P

---

[137] https://www.ebri.org/

[138] https://action.aarp.org/site/Advocacy;jsessionid=F1E44E8318B 09DBC0E63 C314DC544834.app262b?cmd=display&page=UserAction &id=4935&autologin =true&CMP=EMC-SNG-ADV-CON-041815

500 which is fine, but why can't you invest in sectors that are exploding higher like the commodity sector, or other sectors that have been beaten down and cycle theory says are about to reverse higher?

The fact is, employees can and should meet with the human resources department, speak with the plan administrator, and demand change.

What is worse is boomers who are retiring today stay invested in 60% stocks and 40% bonds—what happens if stocks crash again and interest rates rise, causing investors to lose the principal of their bond investments? Bonds have been decimated by the rise in interest rates in the last few years. What happens if we get back to double digit inflation? Rates will rise and bonds will fall.

Is just putting your money into the index funds really the way to manage your money if indeed we see future stock and bond market crashes? What insurance does your portfolio have against this potential scenario?

And finally, the government is proposing to reduce the tax incentives for employers to offer retirement plans to their employees, just as millions of Americans need to start saving more.[139] This is why I am authoring this book so you can take control of your future.

---

[139] http://www.cnbc.com/2014/03/18/obamas-budget-bad-for-401(k)-savers.html

CHAPTER 18 - PROBLEMS FOR THOSE IN RETIREMENT

Those in Retirement Have Other Potential Issues as Well

What about those already in retirement and receiving pensions from their employers? Many of them have seen their benefits reduced and even pension cuts, like those in Detroit had. Many unions across the nation are now outraged because Congress approved a plan to allow pension cuts. This is supposed to keep around 150 pension funds from running out of money.[140]

They are making these cuts naturally to preserve the plans for both retirees and current workers. But after having the stock and bond markets provide phenomenal returns since 2009, the fact that so many pension plans are in trouble now should be alarming. How safe is your pension? What will a future recession or worse do to the financial health of your pension?

Unfortunately, it is worse than many retirees think. They work hard their entire lives and are living a comfortable retirement, and suddenly one day they receive a notice in the mail telling them they will be receiving a 30% or more reduction in payments each month. How outraged would they be? But we will see this increasingly, especially during this next downturn in the markets. Yes, this is true of those who worked for the government too. Governments will always do what is in their best interest to survive. The same goes for social security, if necessary, too.

I was looking at government salaries recently and was alarmed at how much government employees get paid these days. While again this is a subject for another book, and no offense to anyone who is receiving these salaries, but it is unsustainable. And future payments to retirees are unsustainable. You had best put money away into an investment fund just in case there are issues cuts to payments down the road. The Pension Benefit Guaranty Association has been pretty

---

[140] http://money.cnn.com/2014/12/22/retirement/pension-cut/index.html

busy bailing out pensions of late. The last report shows they had $130.9 billion in assets and $86.3 billion in liabilities.[141]

I am not trying to be an alarmist, but I can see how some may think otherwise. I am trying to bring awareness to the public how little control they have over their pension and to start taking control of their future.

For some, it may be wise to retire from their current job and roll over their pension into an IRA where they have control of it. If companies can allow someone to retire and then hire them back the next day, they would be doing their employees a service like no other, but do not expect employers to agree to this. I am always thinking "outside the box" and do not see a reason you cannot ask your employer if there are options for you. This whole book is me thinking outside the box. You will see soon how this outside-the-box thinking can benefit you when I talk about the trading service I offer.

Solutions for Taking Control of Your Retirement

This book is not written to explain all the various pension plans available. Meet with your CFP financial advisor and ask how you can reduce current income taxes by contributing to these plans and whether they fit your situation. I would have to author a 500-page book to include everything there is to know about retiring, including multiple tax strategies, estate planning, charitable planning, and much more, but many would not want to read a book that long. Most want to keep it simple and/or be told what to do. This book, however, has all you need to profit in the future and more.

One critical issue I will address: if you are still working and about to retire, or just retiring, you can roll over (once a year) or transfer (more than once a year) funds from your 401(k) or other retirement accounts from your employer upon retirement.

---

[141] https://www.pbgc.gov/news/press/releases/pr23-048#:~:text=The%20Single%2DEmployer%20Program%20had,%2436.6%20billi on%20a%20year%20earlier.

Alternatives to Retirement:
Living Comfortably Off What You Have Saved

Other solutions for your golden years are to keep working by doing something you enjoy, preferably your own business that gives you many write-offs against your income, and something that makes you happy. Then it is not really considered work and it may just keep your brain and body healthy.

Another idea I will explore in more detail in the *We the Serfs!* book is to simply pack up your things and move to Costa Rica, Ecuador, the Philippines, Portugal or anywhere you can live like a king/queen off your savings or Social Security or whatever small amount of income you might be receiving. In my travels to some of these countries, some of the happiest people I have met have been expats from the United States. They let it be known that they have extra income to enjoy what life offers, even though they would be falling short of that personal fulfillment if still residing in the United States. Relatives can always come to take a vacation and visit you.

There are also states you can move to that might not charge you state taxes, giving your retirement a boost or simply reducing your cost of living. Some states may try to chase you down, however, to get their cut of your taxes they believe is owed them. All states will be hungry for your tax dollars.

Getting to Retirement

You must sacrifice some of the good times now and start saving early for retirement as mentioned. Parents need to instruct their children at an early age about investing and taking control of their future, because our school system has totally missed the boat on this subject. These children need to discuss investing with you as soon as possible and get used to the language of investing. Grandparents, you can do the same thing, especially if you are doing any gifting to children and grandchildren. Get them involved with understanding investments; do not just give them money. In your will you can instruct that to receive the income from an inheritance, they must hold a job. If they are not good at keeping a job, then give them a stream of income through an annuity they cannot outlive. It is better though to try and teach them how to be successful in investing. It is the motivation they need to get through life.

If you do not make this effort to help your children, who will? Most young people will not go out and buy a book on investing or even have a clue about the economy. There is much missing from our "Common Core" education system, and at the top of that list is teaching our youth about money and investing.

PART 4 - CONCLUSIONS FOR
HOW TO PROFIT IN UP AND DOWN MARKETS

CHAPTER 19 - WRAPPING IT ALL UP FOR INVESTORS AND TRADING SERVICE TO MAKE IT SIMPLE

My Goals with This Book

With this book, I have tried to incorporate almost four decades of information, from all the trial and error and discoveries as a financial advisor, planner, and trader. The path I have taken, the good, the bad, the ugly, has led me to bringing this awareness to you, the investor.

The first part of this discussion centered on asking the right questions of those looking to manage your money, because the answers must match your goals for protecting and growing your wealth, not theirs for making commissions. We discussed the performance of those who manage mutual funds and hedge funds and asked whether you could do better investing your money yourself.

We discussed philosophies of investing, ideas of what to look for when investing, and various thoughts on following the money flow of government to know what industries are subsidized where you can earn more profit by investing with those companies. We discuissed trading strategies and what setups to profit from. We discussed how index funds can beat the pros and how you can make money in down markets with inverse ETFs and funds and the ins and outs of when to invest in the trending ETFs. We discussed the importance of gold to preserve purchasing power in a portfolio and alternative asset classes that can perform well moving forward. We undertook a thorough analysis of real estate options, including when to buy and sell. We discussed the life insurance industry and annuities and the pitfalls involved in that industry and why they may make sense for some.

Lastly, we put it all together for those at or near retirement to know what to look out for with their pension plans.

Do not Worry About Your Future, Take Control of It

We provided advice for those who may not be able to retire when they want while also presenting ideas to pursue other avenues that can allow you a better quality of life in retirement.

Our entire political system needs to be overhauled or many of us will simply become serfs if we do not take control of our future. I have worked eighteen years on a forthcoming book called *We the Serfs!* I really do think it can make a difference for all of us in America moving forward. Whether you are from the left or the right point of view, or somewhere in the middle or wherever you may be politically, I want to open this discussion to bring America together for the better. My first three books are the bedrock of understanding for yourself to prepare for what's to come, no matter what that entails. There is no need to fear the unknown with the right understanding of investments as you can truly profit in up and down markets.

Profit in Up and Down Markets Trading Service

When you look at the fees you pay an advisor, they can add up. As an example, with a $100,000 portfolio, most are paying a .25% to 1% fee to an advisor who simply buys an S&P 500 Index fund. This means you are paying $250 to $1,000 a year to someone to manage your portfolio. The fee is based on the total assets under management. The asset management fees you see are illustrated in the following chart of a sample management fee structure.

Total Account Value	Annual Fee	Amount You Pay to Advisor
Up to $50,000	1.45%	$725
$50,001 - $100,000	1.30%	$1,300
$100,001 - $300,000	1.15%	$3,450
$301,000 - $500,000	1.10%	$5,500
$500,001 - $750,000	1.05%	$7,875
$750,001 - $1,000,000	1.00%	$10,000
Next $1,000,000	0.60%	$16,000
Next $1,000,000	0.50%	$21,000
Next $1,000,000	0.40%	$25,000
Next $1,000,000	0.25%	$27,500
Over $5,000,000	Negotiable	Potentially more than $27,500

In authoring my books, I try to bring as much awareness as I can to my readers and challenge the status quo thinking. Most of you can't watch the markets 5-6 hours a day or sit on your hands and do nothing for hours or days. Also, if you were to try and set up your own trading system with all you have learned from this book it would be quite burdensome for many of you. That is why I have done the homework for you by including most everything you have read in this book in one place. I have created a system that provides trade alerts each week that tell you when to buy and when to sell or go short. Once you see the data align it becomes clearer as to when to buy or sell.

Take a look at the following table of SPY, the SPDR S&P 500 ETF Trust. It is all laid out in once screen to give you a snapshot, and you can go back 10 years or more to analyze the data.

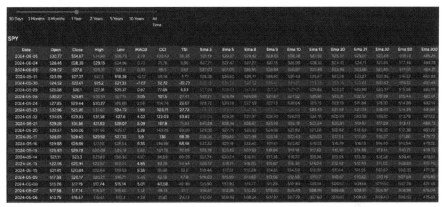

Example of the data you will find. It is difficult to see in print so I have zoomed in on the left half of the table above in the next graphic for readability. The right half are all moving averages to analyze. You can see mostly green as the color in this chart. This tells you to remain bullish SPY at the time this chart is captured. The left half includes SPY prices, MACD, CCI, TSI, all with the proper calculations for setups you found in this book done for you. The right half are the 3,5,8, 9,10,13,20,21,30,50 and 200 day moving averages.

SPY							
Date	Open	Close	High	Low	MACD	CCI	TSI
2024-06-05	530.77	534.67	534.69	528.73	2.79	100.43	30.35
2024-06-04	526.46	528.39	529.15	524.96	0.72	71.76	8.66
2024-06-03	529.02	527.8	529.31	522.6	0.35	69.5	3.92
2024-05-31	523.59	527.37	527.5	518.36	-0.17	59.19	-1.77
2024-05-30	524.52	522.61	525.2	521.33	-1.07	52.72	-12.73
2024-05-29	525.68	526.1	527.31	525.37	0.67	77.65	8.53
2024-05-28	530.27	529.81	530.51	527.11	2.05	101.5	27.41
2024-05-24	527.85	529.44	530.27	526.88	2.08	104.74	26.67
2024-05-23	532.96	525.96	533.07	524.72	1.99	103.71	27.72
2024-05-22	530.65	529.83	531.38	527.6	4.02	123.03	59.83
2024-05-21	529.28	531.36	531.52	529.07	5.09	137.8	71.23
2024-05-20	529.57	530.06	531.56	529.17	5.38	143.25	69.09
2024-05-17	528.81	529.45	529.52	527.32	5.9	136	68.39
2024-05-16	529.88	528.69	531.52	528.54	6.35	146.98	68.58
2024-05-15	525.83	529.78	530.08	525.18	6.62	141.76	70.99
2024-05-14	521.11	523.3	523.83	520.56	4.97	94.89	60.05
2024-05-13	522.56	520.91	522.67	519.74	4.85	82.76	54.64
2024-05-10	521.81	520.84	522.64	519.59	5.36	81.68	52.2
2024-05-09	517.38	520.17	520.21	516.71	5.46	62.18	47.8
2024-05-08	515.26	517.19	517.74	515.14	5.01	40.58	40.98
2024-05-07	517.56	517.14	518.57	516.45	5.12	48.13	37.1
2024-05-06	513.75	516.57	516.61	513.3	4.28	31.82	29.33

What Are the Historical Returns?

The 10 year return for the S&P 500 as of 6/15/2024 was 174.4% compared to 167.3% last month and 156.63% last year. The only years during this period that the S&P experienced losses were 2015, 2018, and 2022, with losses of -0.73%, -6.24%, and -19.44%, respectively. Are you prepared to see your portfolio experience a downturn of any sort when it can be avoided?

The following were the last 10 years' returns for some of the S&P 500 stocks we applied the Profit in Up and Down Markets trading system to. Close to 80% of the stock returns are positive over that time and 20% were negative.

INTC

Total Return: 97.46%
Avg Days in Trade: 274.71
view

U

Total Return: 59.78%
Avg Days in Trade: 245.00
view

MRVL

Total Return: 179.13%
Avg Days in Trade: 297.80
view

GEN

Total Return: 13.58%
Avg Days in Trade: 397.00
view

SQ

Total Return: 139.12%
Avg Days in Trade: 358.75
view

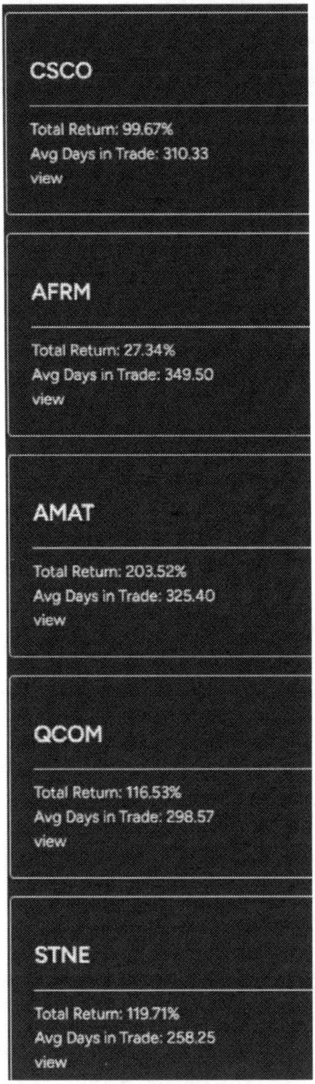

CSCO

Total Return: 99.67%
Avg Days in Trade: 310.33
view

AFRM

Total Return: 27.34%
Avg Days in Trade: 349.50
view

AMAT

Total Return: 203.52%
Avg Days in Trade: 325.40
view

QCOM

Total Return: 116.53%
Avg Days in Trade: 298.57
view

STNE

Total Return: 119.71%
Avg Days in Trade: 258.25
view

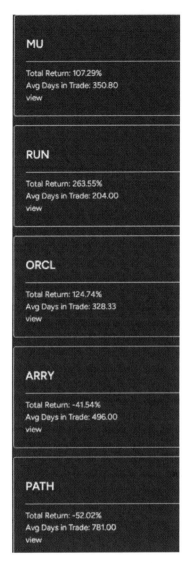

I ran the trading system on all 504 of the S&P stocks and the average return per stock was 83.59% and an average hold of 449.91 days.

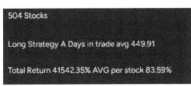

Not only did I analyze the S&P 500 stocks for the last 10 years, but I applied my system to over 1700 stocks that fit the criteria of over $10 a share and volume of over 500,000 shares traded daily and the returns were phenomenal. All of this can be seen on the Profit in Up and Down Markets trading platform website.

The Profit in Up and Down Markets trading system will send alerts on what to buy for the next trading day if there is a buy signal triggered. It will also send out alerts for any sell signals to lock in profit. Lastly, the trading system will send out short signals.

The key to your investing will be to do your own analysis the night before trading and see if the other data we have discussed agrees with the alerts. Remember also, you can take profit anytime you want and wait for the next signal.

The other tools we provide you will find useful for trading. They are a Pivot Point calculator (see sample), access to economic data, Fear and Greed index, heat map of stocks, and the current put/call ratio and VIX analysis. All of these are important to know the market trends and make sure these trends agree with your trades.

Pivot Point Calculator

You will get a Pivot Point Calculator as part of the trading service. With this you can do day trading if you choose to. I will provide the thinkorswim code to use with it. It will look like this. I used QQQ prices in the next graphic for the high, low and close on 6/10 and you put those prices into the calculator. The following charts show that QQQ dipped to the support area between S1 and S2 and Pushed all the way higher to R2 and R1).

The trades you would have made since the first chart shows trend as up (so did the daily chart) was buying the dip at support. You would have bought that dip at the support levels between S1 and S2 with the first buy at S1. We didn't get down to S2 but you may have added either way on a move back up over S1. You would have sold half your position at the first resistance of R1 and possibly the rest at second resistance of R2. You can always let the winner ride longer. These are just pivot point suggestions for day trading. The key is to trade the system and not get greedy. There is always another trade coming. You'll see the low for QQQ on 6/11 was 462.03 and high was 468.14. Close was 468.02. These are the pivots you input into the calculator for the next trading day.

Again, you'll find the settings for the buy arrows you see on the charts in the Pivot Calendar section on the trading service website.

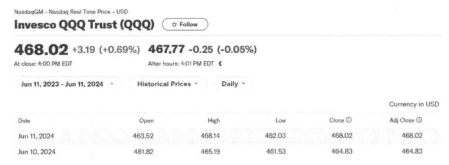

NasdaqGM - Nasdaq Real Time Price • USD

Invesco QQQ Trust (QQQ) ☆ Follow

468.02 +3.19 (+0.69%) **467.77** -0.25 (-0.05%)

At close: 4:00 PM EDT   After hours: 4:01 PM EDT ‹

Jun 11, 2023 - Jun 11, 2024 ⌄   Historical Prices ⌄   Daily ⌄

Currency in USD

Date	Open	High	Low	Close ⓘ	Adj Close ⓘ
Jun 11, 2024	463.52	468.14	462.03	468.02	468.02
Jun 10, 2024	461.82	465.19	461.53	464.83	464.83

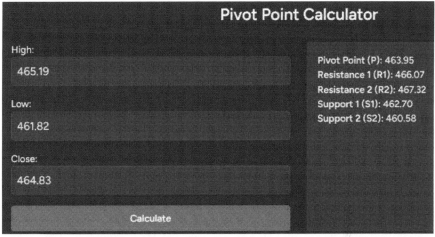

Pivot Point Calculator

High:

465.19

Pivot Point (P): 463.95
Resistance 1 (R1): 466.07
Resistance 2 (R2): 467.32

Low:

461.82

Support 1 (S1): 462.70
Support 2 (S2): 460.58

Close:

464.83

Calculate

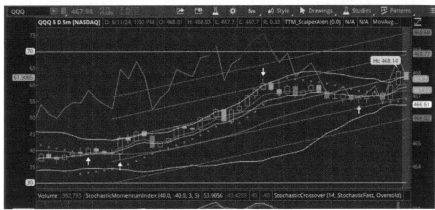

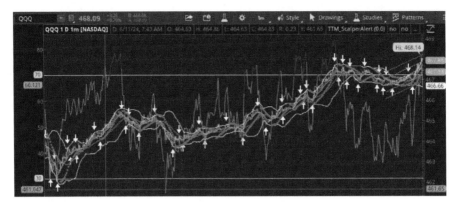

If the stock or ETF is trending down, the pivot calculator provided by the trading service will show a pivot point that you want to short below it with targets of support below for taking profit.

This is all part of the homework you need to do before trading the next day. It's imperative for your trading success. You will be able to view the data applied to over 1700 stocks and view each stock with the data individually as well as many ETF's. These stocks all fit the criteria we applied to qualify as making the grade to trade.

To learn more about the Profit in Up and Down Markets trading system, go to the following website link:
profitinupanddownmarkets.com
The cost for the trading service is $49 a month. If you are going to utilize the trading service I suggest you do so for one year to see how it can transform your outlook on investing and take the fear out of doing so.

Thank you for reading and I wish you the best with your investment decisions moving forward, armed with what you have learned in this book.

Index

1

A

B

C

F

G

M

N

O

P

Q

R

S

T

U

V

W

X

Y

Z

ZeroHedge, 25

Printed in Great Britain
by Amazon

6627c2fa-ede9-4f91-b1bd-b21c228b2784R02